A CHILDHOOD MEMORY BY PIERO DELLA FRANCESCA

Cultural Memory
in
the
Present

Mieke Bal and Hent de Vries, Editors

A CHILDHOOD MEMORY
BY PIERO DELLA FRANCESCA

Hubert Damisch

Translated by John Goodman

STANFORD UNIVERSITY PRESS

STANFORD, CALIFORNIA

2007

Stanford University Press

Stanford, California

English translation © 2007 by the Board of Trustees of the Leland Stanford Junior University. All rights reserved.

A Childhood Memory by Piero della Francesca was originally published in French under the title *Un Souvenir d'enfance par Piero della Francesca*, © 1997, Editions du Seuil.

Assistance for the translation was provided by the French Ministry of Culture.

Printed in the United States of America on acid-free, archival-quality paper

Library of Congress Cataloging-in-Publication Data

Damisch, Hubert.

[Souvenir d'enfance par Piero della Francesca. English]

A childhood memory by Piero della Francesca / Hubert Damisch ; translated by John Goodman.

p. cm.--(Cultural memory in the present)

Includes bibliographical references.

ISBN 978-0-8047-3441-7 (cloth : alk. paper)--ISBN 978-0-8047-3442-4 (pbk. : alk. paper)

1. Piero, della Francesca, 1416?-1492. Madonna del parto. 2. Piero, della Francesca, 1416?-1492--Criticism and interpretation. 3. Mary, Blessed Virgin, Saint--Art. 4. Mural painting and decoration, Renaissance--Italy--Monterchi. 5. Psychoanalysis and art. I. Title.

ND623.F78A755 2007

759.5--dc22   2007007541

Typeset by Bruce Lundquist in 11/13.5 Adobe Garamond

And if you don't mind we'll leave my mother out of all this.

SAMUEL BECKETT, *Molloy*

Contents

List of Figures   xi

Chapter 1   1

Chapter 2   17

Chapter 3   31

Chapter 4   43

Chapter 5   61

Chapter 6   75

Notes   93

Figures

2.1. Piero della Francesca, *Madonna del Parto*   19

2.2. Piero della Francesca, *Madonna del Parto*, detail   24

4.1. Piero della Francesca, *The Annunciation*   49

4.2. A *velarius*, from Daremberg and Saglio,
Dictionnaire des antiquités grecques et romaines   51

4.3. Benozzo Gozzoli, the tabernacle in Exodus   53

4.4. Rogier van der Weyden, *Virgin and Saints*   55

4.5. *Vierge ouvrante*, eastern Prussia, late fourteenth century   57

5.1. *Transformation Mask* from the Pacific Northwest   62

5.2. Albrecht Dürer, *Draftsman Drawing a Nude*   64

5.3. Schema of the first steps of perspective construction
according to Alberti   67

5.4. Piero della Francesca, *De prospectiva pingendi*   69

6.1. Dream of the Wolf Man, after Freud   77

6.2. Piero della Francesca, *Madonna della Misericordia Polyptych*   82

6.3. *Madonna del Parto*: perspective fiction of the beyond   84

A CHILDHOOD MEMORY BY PIERO DELLA FRANCESCA

The title of this essay should suffice as its dedication. Note being taken from the outset, however, of the discrepancy between a reminiscence that has arisen from the depths of the earliest years and a work of painting whose artifice would equal that of a memory of childhood. On one hand, the fable of the supposed vulture that Freud noticed in the writings of Leonardo da Vinci, and that served as his point of departure for the masterpiece of "construction in analysis"—despised by most art historians—that is *Leonardo da Vinci and a Memory of His Childhood*: a book indeed dubious, improbable, but wherein, regardless of what history makes of this construction and its validity, we recognize, to quote Meyer Schapiro (not sparing however in his criticisms), "the hand of a master."[1] And on the other, a work by Piero della Francesca, one whose analytic implications will be measured against the echoes that it can awaken in both individual and collective memory: a "childhood memory," reader please note, not *of* but *by* Piero della Francesca, the emphasis being less on the possessive relation than on the agent.

More is at stake here than a nuance, and it matters all the more because after the fifth centenary of his death, with its attendant celebrations, scholarly gatherings, publications, and restoration work, the name Piero della Francesca calls forth a discursive figure very different from the one that is the gist of Freud's essay on Leonardo da Vinci: the same

Leonardo that Vasari already presented as an artist wracked by doubt, always dissatisfied with himself, and whose major works would bear the stamp of incompletion, his creative faculty having been disturbed, perturbed, even repressed, and perhaps inhibited by an unbridled curiosity or, as Freud writes, by a craving for knowledge (*ein Wissensdrang*), an investigation-drive (*ein Forschungstrieb*, and even *ein Forscherstrieb*: literally, "an investigator-drive") that was ever more consuming and domineering, and that supposedly came to occupy him completely.[2] Whereas today the name Piero della Francesca references not so much a man or a personality as an oeuvre. An oeuvre that, even in its most lacunary and fragile aspects, even in those parts of its precious core that are irremediably threatened, seems to possess a matchless assurance, authority, and determination, and to have no truck with what Freud called "a pattern of not finishing anything."[3] The truth about Piero's Roman work seems hard to establish, apart from some remains discovered in Santa Maria Maggiore in 1913, and that Roberto Longhi was tempted to attribute to him, at least hypothetically (which brings us back, through the idea of a corpus, to the notion of "construction" central to our project).[4] But if the frescoes in Arezzo are gradually fading into a delicately colored haze, the reasons for this are not merely technical, as can be said, by contrast, of the *Battle of Anghiari* or the *Last Supper* by Leonardo: the one having disappeared in the seventeenth century, the other surviving only as traces that are all the more fascinating because, unlike the "hyper-realistic" reconstructions in California's wax museums, they give fantasy free rein.[5]

The brilliance that now emanates from the name Piero della Francesca in the history of art, the clarity, the sense of completion and timelessness that radiate from his work are, however, a bit deceptive. Doubtless linear perspective, which occupied him for so long, was not, at least in its principle, an evening occupation but on the contrary presupposed, for production of the whole of its effect, both the full light of day and a "focused" quality, or at least a clarity of image and a precision of graphic construction that contrasted with the blur of "atmospheric" perspective, the *sfumato* that bathes Leonardo's distant views. To be sure, Piero's figures have the monumental impassability, the paradoxical appearance of archaism associated with an imperious metric, one that seems to renew with a venerable antiquity that Longhi did not hesitate to characterize as "Egyptian" or "Etruscan," and wherein he saw proof of the "underground" persistence of an immemorial figurative tradition whose reemergence at a given moment can coincide with a turning point in the history of artistic creation.[6] We are very far here from the physiognomic enigma of the *Mona Lisa*. And yet Piero's figures, even his compositions, are not without their share of the mystery that often resulted from perspective at its most subtle. And this whether we are dealing with the *Flagellation of Christ* in Urbino, usually dated 1445–1450 (before the great Arezzo cycle), where the rigorous coherence of the geometric construction only increases the eloquence of the marked difference in depth-of-field between the two parts of the scene, thought to correspond to two moments in time, if not to two distinct time periods, that of the gospels and that of contemporary history; with the *Annunciation* in Perugia, where, as pertinent as it ought to be, reconstruction of the floor plan reveals that a compact group of columns oddly interposes itself between the Virgin and the angel of the Annunciation opposite her[7]; or even with the *Montefeltro Altarpiece* in the Brera, one of his last works, contrived such that the egg suspended in the apse seems, if viewed frontally, to be directly above the Virgin enthroned at the crossing of the transept: with the result that what might be an ostrich egg is reduced, as an effect of recession, to the dimensions of a duck egg.[8] Quite apart from the fact that Piero was not just the painter who is familiar to us. The great treatise that he left behind, the *De prospectiva pingendi,* is indeed connected to one of the basic elements of his art; even so, it makes scant reference to painting, evidencing by contrast a passion for geometry and mathematics that is surprising in an artist whom nothing seemed to predispose to such work, and whose oeuvre, after Vasari's time, would not attain its present unmitigated glory until the start of the twentieth century—at the very moment, paradoxically, when modern painting, under the joint protection of Cézanne and cubism, pretended to have dispatched "scientific" perspective.

Freud echoes words that Vasari placed in the mouth of Leonardo da Vinci when, near death and describing the course of his illness with detachment, the latter supposedly expressed regret for having offended God and man by not having worked at his art as he should have[9]—but only to observe immediately thereafter that, despite the improbability of this story (*diese Erzählung*), it was nonetheless invaluable as evidence of what men of that time might have thought about Leonardo. On this point as on others, however, Vasari's text is wholly consistent with the idea that the investigator, the "researcher," clearly prevailed over the artist in Leonardo. Did Freud mean by this that the idea would first have made its way under cover of the legend that began to take shape around Leonardo even during the latter's lifetime, long before Freud took account of it and tried to elucidate the process whereby the investigative drive might come to inhibit an artist's creative power: the analysis offering the example of a subtle transition from an instance of reception to one of production? But if the theme of the artist who is incomparable but too often prevented, for obscure reasons, from bringing his enterprises to completion, if this theme or motif was already present in Vasari, like that of the brake put on the painter's activity by the limitless curiosity that he allegedly manifested from earliest youth, the author of the *Lives of the Painters, Sculptors, and Architects* was nonetheless far from suspecting the extent and systematic character of the investigations undertaken by Leonardo in the most diverse areas; only the publication of his manuscripts, toward the end of the nineteenth century, made it possible to assess this. As Freud emphasizes, "it was left to us to recognize the greatness of the natural scientist (and engineer) that was combined in him with the artist"[10]; and, by the same token, to put the one and the other (the researcher and the artist) on the scales, namely to use them as one would an antagonistic couple whose analysis might have heuristic value. Even so, Vasari was the first to give narrative shape and force to an enigma that, over time, has come to function as a *topos,* a commonplace, a recurrent figure of discourse, and one that took on a new resonance when Freud began to take an interest in Italian art, and more particularly in Leonardo da Vinci, as is evidenced by the many citations found in the little book to which the one you are now reading is dedicated, and more than that: which it takes as its model, and—reader take note—whose form and general organization, including specific turns of phrase and footnotes (not to forget its final paragraph), it deliberately pastiches, in the rather vain hope of reconnecting, through this homage in parodic form, with what constituted its mainspring, its movement, its *impetus* without compare.

In terms of reception, a parallel with the fortune of Piero's art in the first years of the twentieth century presents itself. The painter's oeuvre indeed seems to demand the perspicacity of historians as well as the ingenuity of interpreters. But it doesn't follow from this that its riddle can be solved like a police investigation. Being signed, the Urbino *Flagellation* poses no problem of attribution. The same cannot be said of its iconography; however brilliant, the "solution" that amounts to seeing in it a message addressed by Cardinal Bessarion, by way of Piero, to Federico da Montefeltro, and meant to incite him to embark on a crusade against the Turks throws no light on the operations that, even today, are those of a picture that Montaigne, during his visit to Urbino, got to know in terms that were already the traditional ones.[11] A picture that cannot be regarded only as a historical document, and that demands—a matter of the gaze—something other than a strictly semantic and retrospective approach: if a painting owes everything to the context into which it is born, how are we to understand that it need not lose all its force of attraction, its powers of seduction, once this context has vanished but can remain efficacious until the present that is our own, until the here and now? That is, without ignoring the power of "metamorphosis" dear to André Malraux, the problem of what Marx so aptly called the "eternal charm of Greek art."[12] To say nothing of its "beauty," however understood.

This riddle is intensified, in the matter of Piero's work, by the contrast between the universality that we now tend to ascribe to it and its having been so deeply rooted in an allegedly provincial region. From the sixteenth century, the geographic implantation of the painter's most important creations in an area remote from Tuscany, far from the great metropolitan artistic centers, meant that this work could easily fall into oblivion, despite Vasari's emphatic praise even in the first edition of his *Lives* (Florence, 1550). Vasari, who was himself a native of Arezzo and who could have studied at his leisure the frescoes in San Francesco that Stendhal, when he passed through the city, didn't even glance at. And this, it must be said, despite the objective role that the work could have played precisely because of its seemingly eccentric geographic location: the strategic location of the city of Urbino, with whose destiny his name is linked, on the boundary between the principal power centers of the Italy of the day, and the princely policies inaugurated by Duke Federico da Montefeltro meant that some of the greatest figures of the period could be encountered there, until Bramante and the young Raphael departed for Rome. Not to mention that, as Roberto Longhi showed in 1914, if we accept that there is a connection between the foundations of Giovanni Bellini's style and perspective, then the meeting between the man who must be seen as the father of great Venetian painting and *perspectiva artificialis* as Piero understood it would have taken place in Rimini and Pesaro: that is, in the same atmosphere within which it was given the master of Borgo to carry out the bulk of his activity.[13]

Now it was because of this same perspective, as much as because of the theoretical activity deployed in this domain by Piero della Francesca, that his name, if not his art, would long remain present in memory, and above all in book-based memory. The presence in Urbino of two treatises, one—*De prospectiva pingendi*—dedicated to Federico de Montefeltre and the other—*De quinque corporibus regularibus*—to his son Guidobaldo, was known to specialists. Beginning with a compatriot of the painter, Luca Pacioli, who after profiting from his lessons exhumed the second of these treatises from the ducal library and was so bold as to publish it under his own name after Piero's death, a case of out-and-out plagiarism: as if, not satisfied with usurping the honor due his teacher, he was obliged, as Vasari wrote, to blot out his name[14]— with the result, as Longhi writes (a rapprochement that in the present context takes on a singular relief), that his student's coarsely metaphysical, astrological-Platonic interpretation of his principles seems like an attempt "to turn the genius from Borgo into a magus and holy man along the lines of Leonardo."[15]

Vasari was not alone in denouncing the larceny committed by Pacioli, which he indeed expanded, without providing additional information, to encompass the many books written by Piero before his death. *"E venuto Piero in vichezza ed a morte, dopo avere scritto molti libri"* ("And when Piero grew old and died, after having written many books"): the wording is ambiguous, indicating either that Piero reached an advanced age before writing his books (although another treatise, *Dell'abaco*, dates from at least twenty years earlier), or that he died after having put the finishing touches on them. In 1583, in his preface to *Due regole della prospettiva prattica* by Vignola, Ignazio Danti would still write of the

way Piero del Borgo put regular bodies and other compositions into perspective, despite fra Luca's having taken credit for this[16]: reference to the
painter's scientific activity being in this instance purged of all magical
and metaphysical connotations; as it had been previously in other architectural treatises, for example translations of Vitruvius by Cesariano
(Como, 1521) and by G. B. Caporali (Perugia, 1536), where Piero is classed
among the "moderns," and even in *La Pratica della prospettiva* by Dani-
elle Barbaro (Venice, 1569), who declared Piero's theoretical work out of
date even as he too appropriated part of the text and many of the dia-
grams from *De prospectiva pingendi.*

The oblivion into which the painter's oeuvre subsequently fell
would lift only at the end of the eighteenth century, when the Abbé
Lanzi, at the same time that he accorded Piero a position in the foreground of the Italian artistic landscape, went so far as to compare him
to the Greeks, "who made geometry serve painting."[17] Now it is precisely
this point, the binding together of art and geometry, that should be the
focus of debate: if we set aside the work, often admirable, of scholars
both local and renowned, the ready-made arguments of establishment
critics who judged Piero's art against the measure of "realism" or "naturalism" (until Cézanne and Seurat, Cubism and *pittura metafisica* more
or less explicitly took up the relay), and the growing interest of art-lovers,
connoisseurs (beginning with the great Cavalcaselle), and the art market
in his work, a commonplace that was by no means new imposed itself,
toward the end of the nineteenth century and the beginning of the twentieth, in the ever-growing literature devoted to the painter from Borgo;
from Woltmann, who pronounced Piero's style "petrified [or should we
say: stupefied (*médusé*)?] by scientific knowledge" and judged his technical contribution greater than his artistic one, to Berenson, who said
he felt that the painter was "clogged by his science," and even Adolfo
Venturi, who, while insisting on the historical importance of Piero's
work, opined that in his case "geometric rationales sometimes prevailed
over artistic ones,"[18] this topos returned regularly, and its relation to the
strictly contemporary one that would be Freud's point of departure in
his own analysis of the Leonardo "case" is clear. Not to mention the
Introduction à la méthode de Léonard de Vinci by Valéry, which preceded
it by some twenty years.

The nature of Piero's decided taste for mathematics and geometry nonetheless set it very much apart from the generalized investigative drive that, if we are to believe Freud, ultimately took hold of Leonardo (the same Leonardo, I will return to this elsewhere, who is thought—another critical commonplace, and one that likewise has its history—ultimately to have challenged a perspective system conceived exclusively in graphic and geometric terms so as to make it subordinate to a different regime, one held to be more consistent with the combined physical, physiological, and subjective conditions of vision[19]). None of the above-cited historians or connoisseurs maintain that the theoretical activity that led to the writing of *De prospectiva pingendi* in any way impeded the painter's creative powers; by and large, they tend to think that Piero's art was profoundly impregnated by it. A view strengthened by late nineteenth-century German scholarship on the role of his treatise not only in the history of perspective (if it makes any sense to talk about perspective as an autonomous discipline, and one with its own history[20]) but in the history of science itself, as we now understand the word. But although Piero's contribution to the development of geometry is irreducible to this purely formal aspect (I will have something to say about this farther on), Leonardo Olschki, in his great history of scientific literature in modern languages, notes that Piero was the first to hold forth about a practice—in this instance, painters' perspective, *prospectiva pingendi*—in a way that was strictly deductive, *more geometrico*. A method, as Longhi rightly emphasizes, that would bear fruit not so much with Leonardo as with Galileo and his school: "Olschki rightly perceives that Piero's work brings the empirical era—to which even Brunelleschi and Alberti had fundamentally belonged—to a close, and that it opens the scientific era."[21]

If the theoretician could rightly pretend to so eminent a position, it is easy to see how this might have affected the reception of the artist's work. Julius von Schlosser rightly insisted on the role played in this instance by the teachings of Benedetto Croce.[22] Croce, whose influence on the history of art as long practiced in Italy had two basic features: on the one hand, the prominence accorded to "artistic personalities," in the double sense of subjects and "beacons"—in Baudelaire's sense—of this history, whereas authors such as Riegl and Wölfflin were committed, at least in theory, to a history of art "without artists' names"; and on the other hand, a clear distinction between art, thought to pertain only to the realm of intuition, and science, taken to be limited exclusively to the conceptual order. It matters little that Croce saw art itself as a *sui generis* form of knowledge, and that by opposing the sensible to the intelligible, and intuitive knowledge to conceptual knowledge, he aimed first of all to make a case for "the autonomy of this simpler and more elementary form of knowledge, which has been compared to a dream (to a dream, not sleep) of the theoretical life, with respect to which philosophy would be the waking state"[23]: hence the "alogical" character ascribed to art, if it is true that intuition no more distinguishes between reality and fiction than dreams do, and that it sticks with a notion of the image as pure ideality, without attaining to the concept. Just as it matters little that he was not afraid to emphasize the superiority of artistic doctrines that he called "conceptualist," beginning with those of Schelling and Hegel, which tended to conflate art with religion, philosophy, and even, in the case of Herbart's followers, mathematics: as the author of the *Breviario d'estetica* notes, these doctrines not only manage to acknowledge the *theoretical* character of art; "they also make their own contribution to the true doctrine, thanks to their demand for a determination of the relations (which, if relations of difference, are also those of unity) between fantasy and logic, between art and thought."[24] By and large, what was retained from Croce, more than the idea of a possible communication with or even an alliance between the realms of art and science, was the notion that the scientific spirit and, more subtly, the mathematical spirit (insofar as this could boast of creating a universe of *fictions,* close in this regard to that of art, but at the cost of abandoning all modalities of inscription save abstract ones) were sworn enemies of the "poetic" spirit.

If one holds that the richest periods for the natural sciences and mathematics are also the ones least fruitful for everything pertaining to "poetry," what then to say about a rivalry that, within a single "artistic personality," pits the geometer against the artist? Especially as perspective, issuing as it did from a fundamentally architectonic intention, is decidedly on the side of science. Art, Croce writes further, can be "constructed physically," as likewise applies in the field of science, only on condition that the analyst (and the artist) free himself from esthetic response and divert his attention from its proper object.[25] Whence the question, as Schlosser posed it: Setting aside all problems of style and history, what is it that constitutes the central and innermost essence (*seinem innersten und centralen Wesen nach*) of Piero della Francesca as artist?[26] Or to put the thing differently, in terms more likely to hold our attention here: How does Piero compare, precisely as *artist,* with the two figures taken to be emblematic of the two key moments of the Renaissance—that of its first theoretical affirmation and that of the crisis of its maturity—who are on the one hand Leone-Battista Alberti, and on the other Leonardo da Vinci? Alberti, whose work on perspective and geometry Piero would carry on in his fashion, and who according to a commonplace dating from the same Schlosser is regarded as a rhetorician cut off from studio practice, but who nonetheless recognized the inaugural import of Brunelleschi's ideas and set about popularizing them, even (another commonplace) codifying them[27] (whereas *Della Pittura* comes across to attentive readers, notably in the connection and even equivalence it posits between art and science, as one of the founding texts of Western culture). And Leonardo da Vinci, who is inscribed in the immediate aftermath of Piero (he had reached forty by the time Piero died), the connection between the two artists having been established by Luca Pacioli, who introduced into Leonardo's studio the manuscript of the treatise on regular bodies: the same Leonardo whose *Künstlerschaft,* or creative power, supposedly was repressed (the Freudian theme is unmistakable) by his multifaceted scientific research, tragically left in a fragmentary state, as would be (I quote Schlosser) his artistic oeuvre.[28]

Stated in these terms, the question echoes the alternative that Benedetto Croce thought summed up the discourse of art criticism: either something is a work of art, or it is not a work of art. We are familiar with the importance in twentieth-century avant-garde culture, notably as operative in the work of Marcel Duchamp, of the marked difference between art and non-art. The fact that Croce, from the beginning of the century, saw this as the point of departure for an esthetic is sufficient indication that the distinction at issue is not necessarily of a purely nominal order, nor esthetics reduced to nominalism.[29] What we must speak of in this instance is not a difference but a boundary, the problem finally making complete sense only where and when the said boundary seems to pass not so much between art and non-art as through a given work, even a given "personality," raising by the same token the question of the "essence"—artistic or non-artistic—of its activity. Schlosser would see this as warrant to proclaim Alberti's equivocal essence "non-artistic" (because "rhetorical"), judging him to be more "sophist" than "human-ist."[30] And likewise, forgetting Leonardo but as a good reader of Vasari, to see Paolo Uccello as a typical example of a painter whose cultivated passion for perspective led him away from the paths alleged to be those of painting. In fact, it was singularly to simplify his task, as regards Piero, to appeal to the equivalence between art and science marked by the Renaissance in its beginnings (but soon rejected, preeminently by Vasari), and to seek confirmation of this in the person of Goethe, in whom the poet supposedly was on equal footing with the man of science.[31] Even if the argument of the theoretician by no means cast light on the practice of the artist, we would still have to determine how, in the optic that would be Vasari's, the double vocation of the man Longhi called a "Janus of painting and science"[32] managed to realize itself in a most singular and harmonious fashion, without one aspect of his activity compromising the other—indeed, quite the contrary—whereas the example of Leonardo, like that of Paolo Uccello, seemed to weaken this optimist scenario. For Vasari himself had to admit something that, in the context of his *Lives,* looks like a paradox: despite the violence that fra Luca (Pacioli) did to Piero by seeking to obliterate his name, even to blot it out (*cerco d'annullare il nome*), and by usurping the honor due the man from whom he had learned everything, the master's theoretical writings preserved in Borgo could not help but increase the glory of one who, "having been held a rare master of the difficulties of drawing regular bodies, as well as of arithmetic and geometry, was [also] excellent in painting."[33] So true is it that renown [*renommée*] is never more assured, as indicated by its etymology, than when it proceeds from a reiterated inscription of a name—in the field of science as well as, in this instance, in that of art.

The paradox was sufficiently great—and the problem sufficiently complex—for tradition to work constantly, if not to resolve it then at least to displace it, by fabricating the legend of a Piero who became blind late in life and, no longer able to devote himself to his art, was reduced to speculating. We find the beginnings of such a legend in Vasari himself, who has it that Piero was prevented from publishing the results of his work, even before his death, by the blindness that overtook him in old age[34]: a blindness whose strictly physical character is underlined by the author of the *Lives* (*la cecità corporale*), as if to indicate that it did not compromise, in this "good old man," the exercise of his intellectual faculties. The legend would grow stronger with the passage of time, but not without continuing to play on the opposition between light and darkness. In 1556, sixty-four years after the painter's death, another old man by the name of Martin di Longaro, a maker of "lanterns for walking about at night," would report to Berto degli Alberti a memory of his first youth that the latter duly transcribed in the little notebook into which he consigned his memoirs: "When he was little, the said Marco used to lead about by the hand Mastro Piero dila [sic] Francesca, an outstanding painter who had gone blind: this is what he told me."[35]

If there was (corporal) blindness, Piero would have suffered from it only in the very last years of his life; Giorgio Mancini set out to prove that the manuscript of *De quinque corporibus,* written by Piero (to quote the dedication) "*in extremo aetatis suae calculo*" (when his days were running out) and preserved in the Vatican, is indeed from his hand, later extending the demonstration to the Parma manuscript of the *De prospectiva pingendi.*[36] Now the same scholar discovered, in notarial records preserved in the State Archives in Florence, an autograph draft of the will written by Piero and set down by *ser* Mario Fedeli on July 5, 1487, five years before the painter's death.[37] Quite apart from the fact that everything suggests that *De prospectiva pingendi* was drafted much later in the artist's career than had generally been thought, and that far from being the fruit of the enforced leisure of an elderly master prevented from exercising his art by the infirmities of old age, this treatise is the most complete product of the theoretical work that was a constant and obligatory counterpoint to the work of painting as the master of Borgo conceived it.[38]

Here again, Vasari set the tone:

Piero applied himself in his youth to mathematics, and although it was settled when he was fifteen years of age that he was to be a painter, he never abandoned this study; nay, he made marvelous progress therein, as well as in painting. He was employed by Guidobaldo Feltro the elder, Duke of Urbino . . . there were preserved there some of his writings on geometry and perspective, in which sciences he was not inferior to any man of his own time, or perchance even to any man of any other time; as is demonstrated by all his works, which are full of perspectives, and particularly by a vase drawn in squares and sides, in such a manner that the base and the mouth can be seen from the front, from behind, and from the sides; which is certainly a marvelous thing, for he drew the smallest details therein with great subtlety, and foreshortened the curves of all the circles with much grace.[39]

And also this, in reference to the plagiarism committed by Luca Pacioli:

Piero, as it has been said, was a very zealous student of art, and gave no little attention to perspective; and he had a very good knowledge of Euclid, insomuch that he understood all the best curves drawn in regular bodies better than any other geometrician, and the clearest elucidations of these matters that we have are from his hand.[40]

"*Studiosissimo dell'arte*": the phrase is apt. For the problem is not in fact so much one of knowing how the artist and the geometer—or to use Croce's language, intuition and concept—managed to coexist so well in Piero, and how his passion for painting could accommodate his taste for mathematics. Any more than it is, exclusively, a matter of assessing the cost to the painter of rationales developed in a deliberately deductive way. What's in question, before all else, is to understand how, associating as he did the practice of painting with reflection on the conditions of its exercise, Piero was able to bring himself to write a treatise that most art historians don't quite know what to do with, but that must be taken seriously by the history of science. If it is true that the perspective specific to painters, *prospectiva pingendi*, was not reducible for Piero to a simple technique in the service of painting, and that the rationales to which it lent itself should, in his mind, issue in a theory of proportions, the mere fact of his having begun by treating it in terms of strict geometry, and essentially plane geometry, in view of preparing a transition to arithmetic, in the guise of numerical progressions corresponding to the regular diminution of figures as an effect of distance, shows sufficiently that, beyond the "artistic significance" (to quote Longhi) rightly attributable to him, *De prospectiva pingendi* bears witness to the speculative power that can accrue to art when it is governed by a paradigm that is as strong as the perspective paradigm. The remark holding, *mutatis mutandis,* for contemporary art in its relation to color, and for what might be its "geometry"—but then, according to Roberto Longhi, couldn't Piero's style be summed up as a synthesis of form and color warranted by perspective, insofar as the painter did not use it to strictly illusionist ends?[41]

It was all very well for Croce to distinguish between art and science, to oppose intuition to concept, and to recognize in the mathematical a sworn enemy of the spirit that he called poetic. Just as Vasari never stopped stripping perspective of its speculative aura so as to reduce it to a simple matter of craft, a purely technical problem, pretending all the while, in Piero's case, not to regard art and science, painting and geometry as antithetical. Long before Freud and Schlosser, the "Life of Paolo Uccello" introduced, by the detour of a justly famous fable, the topos of the artist who is a victim of his limitless passion for this science, to the point of abandoning his conjugal bed[42]: the fable taking on all the more relief because the *scrittoio,* or study, in which the painter supposedly shut himself up to pursue his studies of perspective was also the place where the head of the family kept the *care iscritture,* the precious writings that, in the form of family registers, served as memory of the family line: a "secret Bluebeard's chamber," to quote Christiane Klapisch-Zuber, "an exclusively masculine space prohibited to the wife,"[43] but where perspective—also an exclusively masculine thing?—apparently had its place. The "artistic personality" of Piero such as Longhi undertook to *construct* it (I emphasize this word advisedly because it bears directly, as I have said, on my argument here), as much as the one that constituted the "essence" of his art for Schlosser, undoes all dichotomies of this kind. Longhi saw well that the notion of Piero's having been a prisoner of science betrayed what was, on Berenson's part, an outmoded attachment to a romantic conception of inspiration. But it is not enough to note that in Piero's and Leonardo's day the boundary between art and science was not where we would tend to draw it today, and that these words did not then have quite the same meaning as they do now. The fact that one and the same man could paint *The Legend of the Wood of the Cross,* produce in *Dell'abaco* an algebraic model for the commercial calculations of his day,[44] and dedicate to the Duke of Urbino the great book on geometry that is *De prospectiva pingendi* is sufficient indication of the circulation, displacements, operations, and transpositions (exemplified by the transition from perspective to geometry) as well as, simultaneously, of the deflections and short-circuits of all sorts that might be active in a work [*travail*] wherein abstraction contends with representation, concept with intuition, color with form, and—to use Freud's language—investigation with creation. All of this being caught up in a permanent exchange of roles comparable—to take Croce's text literally—to what can happen in dreams.

But there is another feature, one whose character is more strictly biographical, that would justify the parallel we might be tempted to establish between "Piero the man" and "Leonardo the man"—-on the tacit understanding that under this title or moniker we are dealing, yet again, with two mental abstractions or constructions, whether conceived in historical or analytic terms, as would also be the case, still on Freud's part, for "Moses the man." The same Vasari to whom we are indebted for having introduced into the artistic literature the topos of the opposition between art and science gave the artist's mother, in his life of Piero, a role analogous, although in a precisely opposite sense, to the one Freud thought he could assign to that of Leonardo da Vinci. Like the natural child Leonardo, who Freud says spent the first years of his life with his mother only to be taken away from her when he was between three and five years old, and welcomed at his grandfather's residence by his young and tender stepmother, who was childless, Vasari affirms, as early as the second paragraph of his life of Piero, that the latter was raised by his mother, whose name he took, his father having died before his birth, leaving his wife pregnant. The author of the *Lives* going so far as to maintain that the mother, despite being a widow, helped her son attain to the rank that his good fortune held out to him.[45]

Even though the investigative drive whose development might have been fostered by the father's absence took a very different course than it did in Leonardo and in no way impeded his creative power—indeed, quite the contrary—the temptation to apply the Freudian schema to Piero would be great, if this were not a fable that is itself dubious. As to this point, modern scholarship has reset the clocks, so to speak: we now know that the father, Benedetto, did not die until February 1464 and that he was buried in the family vault, in the Badia of Borgo (the present cathedral), in the same place where Piero himself would ask to be buried in his will. Far from having been a solitary orphan, the painter had at least two brothers and a sister, although it is not altogether clear whether he was the eldest, as Longhi suggests.[46] Although he may have remained single, the powers of attorney that he signed in favor of one of his brothers as well as his own will prove that despite his repeated absences he had his place in Borgo within the family clan. And as for the mother, a native of the town of Monterchi, near Borgo, and who answered to the name not of Francesca but of Romana, the *Libro dei Morti* indicates that she died on November 6, 1459, which was five years before her husband.[47] Regarding Piero's relations with her, we are reduced, having set aside the fable of the father's death and a strictly maternal education, to what Vasari indicates and to what the documents seemingly confirm: namely, that after having worked in Rome the painter returned to Borgo after the death of his mother (*"essendo morta la madre"*[48]). As Freud writes at the end of the first chapter of his essay on Leonardo da Vinci: *"Das ist alles"*—that is all.

Personal remarks are wholly absent from Piero's theoretical writings, but the painted oeuvre offers another trail distinct from that of archival documents. In the corpus of paintings ascribed to him, at least one fresco—unknown to Vasari—has a direct relation to the maternal world. And a relation all the more close, if not intimate, because, taking Vasari at his word, it is tempting to think that Piero painted it precisely on his return from Rome, in the years following his mother's death, and by the same token to see here a kind of implicit homage to her; but without excluding the possibility that he might have worked on it while Monna Romana was still living, if one accepts the earlier dating proposed by Longhi on purely stylistic grounds, or by contrast a date long after her death as maintained by Eugenio Battisti, who likewise relies on stylistic evidence while introducing liturgical considerations that he thinks are very important,[1] but that nonetheless do not suffice to explain the presence, some distance from Borgo San Sepolcro, on the outskirts of the little fortified town of Monterchi that was Monna Romana's birthplace, of a masterpiece so unexpected, due as much to its subject as to the painter's treatment of it. Unless, the one not excluding the other, the maternal relatives took advantage of the renown of the painter from Borgo to obtain this commission for him, one all the more singular because the detachment of the *Madonna del Parto* in 1910 revealed the existence, under Piero's work, of another fourteenth-century fresco, one whose surviving fragments—a head of the Virgin, part of a hand, the head of a child, and that of an angel—indicate that it was a Virgin and child accompanied by one or more angels: the question then becoming one of determining why it was deemed good at the time to substitute for this widely disseminated medieval image (although its already having been venerated under the sign of childbirth cannot be excluded) an image much more rare and problematic.[2]

An image, what's more (since this inquiry is itself inscribed under the rubric of a childhood memory), related not only to maternity but to filiation. And this in the guise most likely to make an impression at the time. Beginning with the local population, as is indicated by a description cast in the style and vocabulary of the art-historical vulgate: the Virgin, dressed in a long blue robe, very simple in appearance, unbuttoned in front and at the sides to make herself comfortable, and allowing the white fabric of the undergarment to show, this Virgin, her carefully depilated face under a golden halo (but does this feature—depilation—accord with the appearance of the dress, regularly qualified as "rustic," if not of the female figure?), her left hand placed on her hip while the fingers of her right one brush lightly against the long vent that opens in the dress at the level of the belly whose swell is thereby accentuated, stands under a tent-like dais whose flaps are held open by two angels placed on either side; the symmetry being all the more pronounced because the last two figures were quite obviously traced mechanically using a single cartoon that was simply reversed, the alternately hot and cold tones of their wings, robes, and hose opposing one another two-by-two (although this could be the result of time and of successive restorations): pink and green for the wings, green and purplish-blue for the robes, red and green for the hose.

In addition to the presence of numerous repaintings, the restoration recently completed by Guido Botticelli has confirmed that part of the feet of the two angels and all of the calotte of the tent are later reworkings whose degree of conformity to the original, at least as regards the hemispherical cover of the dais, cannot be determined. The restorer's report does not mention the traces of painting visible to either side of the tent, outside of it, which some have seen as proof that

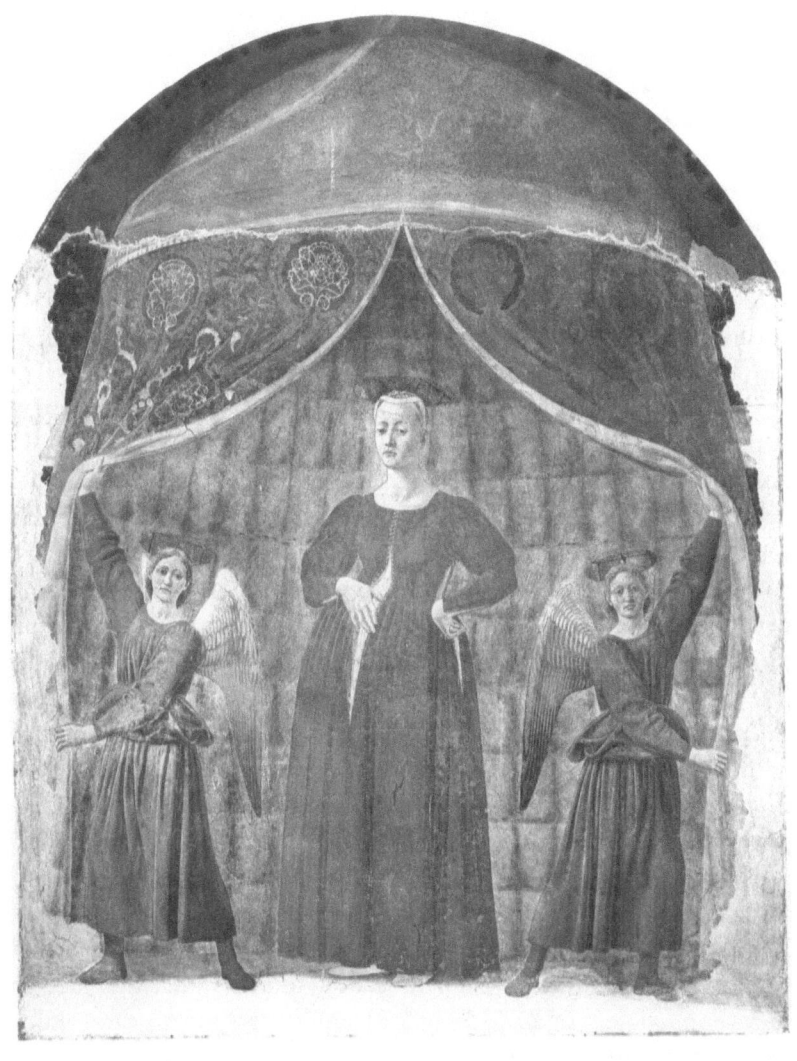

2.1. Piero della Francesca, *Madonna del Parto*, Monterchi. Photo © Alinari-Giraudon.

the ensemble constituted by the dais and the figures within it stood out against a smooth wall, treated as a background of polychrome faux marbre, in accordance with a principle known from other frescoes from the Quattrocento.[3] By contrast, it specifies that the *intonaco* made of whitewash and sand was applied in seven "days" of successive work, in varying sizes, proceeding from top to bottom, the drawing having been transferred to the support, using the *polvero* process, with great care and attention to detail, as is evidenced in particular by the embroidered vegetal decoration of the tent's exterior.[4] To say nothing of the black outline, scarcely emphasized but quite visible and traced at one go, of the face and neck.

With the exception of Kenneth Clark and, above all, Ingeborg Walter,[5] most historians have been curiously loath to admit a connection of any kind between the Monterchi fresco and the artist's mother (which, as we shall see, changes nothing about the matter, objectively speaking). Others (in fact not very many) have gone so far as to cast doubt on its being, in whole or in part, a work by Piero. Beginning with Berenson, who, following Cavalcaselle, attributed its execution to a certain Lorentino d'Andrea, mentioned by Vasari as one of the few followers of the painter from Borgo. In fact, the fresco in Monterchi has always been considered a work apart. First of all in geographic terms, because of the doubly remote position that it occupied—"*fuor della terra,*" as Vasari writes about some frescoes that Piero supposedly painted in Santa Maria delle Grazie, at the gates of Arezzo[6]—until recently at the back of a chapel of modest dimensions, without architectural character, situated halfway up a hillside facing the *castello* of Monterchi. The grapevine mixed with wisteria that, during my first visits, formed a vault over the path leading to it has since disappeared to accommodate a small parking lot happily off-limits to cars, which made it necessary for the hordes of tourists to climb the hill on foot and thus retained the pilgrimage-like character of the visit.[7] Alas, things are no longer the same today, the fresco having been moved into the village school and installed—like the *Nefertiti* in the Egyptian museum in Berlin, but in a less luxurious context more redolent of a modest movie theater—surrounded by darkness, within a luminous glass box that, far from functioning like a reliquary and restoring some semblance of aura to the image, makes it look like a hologram, if it isn't reduced to a derisory beaker containing a rare specimen that in this context takes on the allure of an iconographic curiosity.[8]

The chapel to which it is to be hoped the fresco will soon be returned is all that survives, after many modifications, of a church mentioned in the thirteenth century under the name Santa Maria di Momentana, but that the official accounts of the regular visits of the bishops of Borgo to Monterchi indicate was also called Santa Maria in Silva. A sanctuary itself of modest dimensions, and which had only two altars: the main altar, erected in the choir and behind which was Piero's fresco; and another altar situated in an open niche in the left wall of the nave, at the back of which, protected by a wooden grille, was enclosed a statue of the Virgin and child made of wood, flanked by two paintings representing Saint Augustine and Saint John the Evangelist and surmounted by an Annunciation. The devotion long directed toward this statue led the authorities of Monterchi to take special care of this ensemble, to the point of establishing around 1580 an *opera della Madonna di Momentana,* charged with administering the offerings of the faithful. As for Piero's fresco, although initially it might have received special attention, we know that at the end of the sixteenth and until the eighteenth century its corresponding altar was abandoned, the focus of the cult having shifted to the Madonna and child. But even this devotion must have been on the decline, for the church finally took the name of *San Agostino,* whose cult might long have been associated with that of Mary, as is suggested by the presence of an image of the saint beside the Virgin and child— until 1785, when the gonfalonier and representatives of the community of Monterchi requested authorization to demolish part of the building to build a new cemetery. To which the bishop consented, on condition that the commune undertake to maintain the cemetery chapel, and without any mention being made on this occasion of Piero's fresco, which seems to have escaped destruction only as an economy measure: proceeding in the most expeditious way, the demolition brought down the nave of the church but left its choir, to which the present chapel corresponds, despite radical transformations effected in 1956 with the intention of isolating it from the cemetery, and which above all changed its orientation.[9]

Shall we dispense with the term *momentana,* "momentary"? In fact, the adjective attached to the statue of the Virgin and child is just the name of a stream that runs through the area. As for *in silva,* this expression traditionally designated a place that was deserted, wooded, wild (classical Latin: *silva*): a place that was *other,* remote, like the one to which the Virgin retired just before giving birth. The *Vergine Partoriente,* as it was designated in the records of pastoral visits, where—a fact rare enough to be noteworthy—the painter's name is sometimes mentioned[10]: proof, at the very least, that even after the council of Trent Piero's masterpiece was not forgotten and that the bishops themselves were able to recognize its beauty, despite the pall of suspicion that many claim was cast over images and even icons of this kind by the Counter-Reformation.[11] Subsequently, mentions become rarer and less laudatory, trace of the work gradually being lost. In 1828, Bishop Annibale Tommasi indicates that during his visit to Monterchi the antiphon of the most blessed Virgin was sung in the church of the *campo santo,* under the title "Expectancy of childbirth," along with its prayer[12]: except that although the prelate mentions the altar, "which was as it should be," he ignores the work by Piero. So things would continue until 1889, when an engineer by the name of Vincenzo Funghini, come from Arezzo to examine an old well, and whom the mayor invited to see the fresco (apparently still present in people's minds), cried out, after having scarcely entered the chapel: "*È Piero della Francesca!*"[13] The next year, a functionary of the administration of cultural property was sent to the place, having been charged with drafting a preliminary report on the image of the "maternity of Mary," otherwise named—for the first time?—the *Madonna del Parto,* attributed to Piero della Francesca.[14]

However original, and in all respects surprising, Piero's *Madonna del Parto* is nonetheless not unique of its kind. It belongs to an iconographic type that appeared in the fourteenth century in Italy and of which several fifteenth-century examples are known. This type, itself not without precedents, would enjoy a certain vogue until the eighteenth century, if not in Italy itself then at least in Germany, Spain, Portugal, and even South America, where it is known as the "Madonna de l'O" (the "O" in question corresponding to the interjection with which the antiphons of the Virgin begin), which suffices to demonstrate that the council of Trent did not ban it, as some maintain without adducing further proof.[15] The appellation itself, which would seem to have been applied to Piero's work for the first time when it was rediscovered, at the end of the nineteenth century, is of older origin, and not without its equivocal aspect: there was venerated in Rome, in the church of San Agostino, under the title of *Madonna del Divin Parto,* a sculpted group from the hand of Sansovino that is in fact a seated Virgin and child, the latter already old enough to sit up on his mother's knees, the image in fact owing its ritual title to its ongoing worship by pregnant women.

Opposed to what would perhaps better be called the *Madonna Post Partum* was an image of "Tuscan" type whose *ante partum* look or aspect is more or less pronounced or obvious: a standing Virgin in a long dress and very ample cape, and shown, with a few exceptions, in three-quarter view and full-length, wearing a girdle and holding on her belly, whose manifest swell is to be taken as a sign of pregnancy, a book that would be, in the fourteenth century, simultaneously a symbol of the incarnate Word and a canonical attribute of the *Madonna del Parto.* The known examples, which are few, in Florence and its immediate environs, all small panels that have none of the amplitude of the Monterchi fresco, scarcely differ from one another save in the background against which the figure stands out—whether this be a solid neutral ground, a feigned architectural niche, or a dais-like tapestry supported by two angels—and in the gesture, described as "chaste," whereby the Virgin sometimes pulls one of the panels of her cape to the level of her lower belly or plays with the cords of her girdle.[16] When, that is, the image of the so-called *Regina coeli* type, wearing crown, halo, and starry mantle, her feet resting on a crescent moon, does not combine with that, pacified for the purpose at hand, of the Apocalyptic Woman.[17]

The image of the pregnant Virgin is also encountered in other guises, older and more widespread but belonging to a single iconographic group: beginning with that of the *Visitation*—the meeting between Mary and Elizabeth—in which each of the protagonists confirms by touch the reality of the very visible pregnancy of the other; to say nothing of *Annunciations* in which the Virgin stands upright, already in a majestic pose befitting the mother of Christ—as with Piero's Virgin in the Arezzo *Annunciation,* and in the effective presence of the two first

Persons of the Trinity, the Father and the Holy Spirit, as well as in that, implicit, of the third Person. But whatever the later fate of the image of the *Madonna del Parto*—for example in colonial Brazil, where Nossa Senhora do Ó (Our Lady of Expectancy) was worshiped in the guise of a pregnant woman, and where sterile women, their petticoats raised, rubbed themselves against the legs of São Gonçalo do Amarante, as was quite consistent with the project of population growth with which the Catholic Church reluctantly became associated[18]—Piero's Virgin stands apart, beyond its specifically pictorial quality and its monumental aspect, because of a gesture that was unprecedented, although it too has an equivocal side. Eugenio Battisti saw in this image something like an autodeictic transformation of the Virgin of the Visitation.[19] But the gesture in question has implications other than purely indicative ones. Implications that, whatever their theological or "Marian" resonances,[20] bear directly on the question of the "childhood memory."

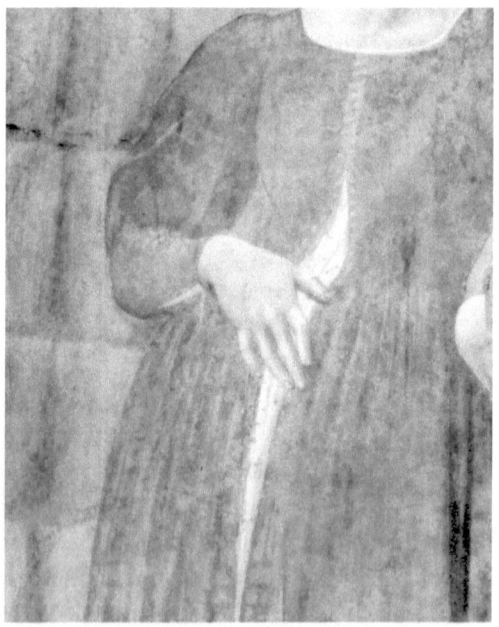

2.2. Piero della Francesca, *Madonna del Parto*, detail.

In this connection, we need only consider the way the fingers of the hand on the belly play over the vent of the dress and seem to insinuate themselves into the folds of the chemise, reconnecting by the same token, without there being any need for a pointed index finger, with what Freud called "the oldest and most burning question that confronts immature humanity": *Where do babies come from?*[21] A riddle-question, as he himself called it,[22] which he saw echoed in countless myths, tales, and legends, and first in the riddle put to Oedipus by the Theban Sphinx.[23] But also in the Christian mystery of the Incarnation, although the question, in this instance, has less bearing on where babies come from than on *how they get in there,* and *who puts them there:* Freud going so far as to see in the craving for knowledge (the *Wissensdrang*) that comes to light in the young child when he "comes to be occupied with the first, grand problem of life," and in the intellectual rumination that thenceforth accompanies his investigations, as well as in the doubts awakened in him by the evasive answers, reprimands, and fables that are supposed to satisfy his curiosity, the prototype of all subsequent work of thought aiming to solve riddles that might be of a very different order.[24] The craving for knowledge characteristic of all small children, their untiring love of asking questions, remaining a riddle for the adult so long as he fails to understand that they are merely circumlocutions (detours), and that they cannot come to an end because the child is only trying to make them take the place of a question that matters to him but that he does *not* ask.[25]

One recognizes here the thesis that, two years later, would make up the argument of "Leonardo da Vinci and a Memory of His Childhood" (the same Leonardo whose artistic personality already constituted for his contemporaries another kind of riddle): if the force of the drive managed to transpose itself within the artist into many forms, to the point that investigation finally took the place of creation for him, that is because his libido escaped the fate of repression through the detour of sublimation,[26] Leonardo having been all the more precociously tormented by "the great question of where babies come from and what the father has to do with their origin"[27] because he had to face up, in early childhood, to an additional problem—namely, the absence of the father. If we are to believe Freud's interpretation of the childhood memory that was recounted by Leonardo (or that he echoed by appropriating for himself what was, according to Schapiro, a commonplace in the literature of the time), and according to which a bird (a vulture, as Freud thought because he read it in Herzfeld—"happy mistake," as Lacan dared to call it[28]—or more prosaically a kite), having descended into his cradle, opened his mouth with its tail and beat his lips with it several times, we must conclude that after his illegitimate birth he was raised by his mother, poor and abandoned, before being received into his father's household around the age of four or five: too late, that is, for the impressions of first infancy to have lost their meaning under the influence of later experience. The day Leonardo learned, through his reading, that the Egyptians had chosen the vulture as a symbol of maternity because they believed this species to consist, as could be read in the *Hieroglyphica* of Horapollon, exclusively of females that the wind impregnated (scarabaeus beetles being venerated by the same Egyptians because all of them were reputedly male), there would have arisen within him this memory indicating that he too had been a vulture-child, a child who had had a mother but no father: with which was associated, "in the only way in which impressions of so great an age can find expression, an echo of the pleasure he had had at his mother's breast."[29] Freud does not stop there, however, going on to recall that the fable of vultures impregnated by the wind figured among the arguments used by the Fathers of the Church to confront those who doubted the miraculous conception of Christ through an operation of the Holy Spirit.[30] Hence the subsequent development of what seems like a product of imagination:

The allusion made by the Fathers of the Church to the representation [*Vorstellung*] of the Blessed Virgin and her child—an image cherished by every artist—must have played its part in helping the fantasy to appear valuable and important to him. Indeed in this way he was able to identify himself with the child Christ, the comforter and savior not of this one woman alone.[31]

But why introduce, with regard to the *Madonna del Parto*, the idea or concept of the "childhood memory"? If we set aside the other fable invented by Vasari—that of the father's having died before the child's birth and having left the task of raising him to his wife—we know nothing about Piero della Francesca's childhood. And as for the man that he was, we scarcely know more than his name: that of the author, attested or presumed, of a certain number of paintings and of some treatises of scientific aspect; and also the one (the name) that scholars have found in books where births and deaths were recorded, in contracts executed with patrons, in tax ledgers and notarial archives. A single feature being worthy of note: the close connection with his region of origin, around which is organized the circulation that would have led the painter first to Florence, in his years of apprenticeship (Florence, to which he would never again return), then to Rimini, Ferrara, Rome, Ancona, Arezzo, and of course Urbino, but likewise to Monterchi, in the immediate environs of Borgo San Sepolcro. Nothing, either in the paintings or in the writings to which his name is attached, seems to offer the slightest access to what we must call his "unconscious," if this notion has any meaning at all here. Nothing, if not perhaps this Virgin who is enclosed under this dais, in a radical withdrawal or isolation that the two symmetrically traced angels who make up her cortege do not suffice to populate. Nothing, if not this monumental figure that is upright, erect, and in a word phallic. Nothing, if not this gesture that is scarcely one, and that is taken to be chaste, but with which the image nonetheless seems implicitly to answer the question which is that of the "young humanity" about which Freud speaks, designating as she does the very place through which the fruit that the woman so obviously carries within her womb will soon pass. To say nothing (and here we come to what is without any doubt the essential thing) of the *construction* that gives all its meaning to the image and even to the gesture, which, it bears repeating, is without precedent.

In Freudian terms, a literally premature death of the father would accord quite well with the hypothesis that this maternal image might be able to shed some light on the deepest strata of Piero's oeuvre, in the way Freud thought that he could conclude from Leonardo's childhood fantasy, and from the substitution of the vulture for the mother, that the child felt deprived of his father and lonely with his mother—something that none of the rare surviving documents concerning his childhood confirm. As to the death of the father, this was, as we saw, pure fabulation on Vasari's part, but a fabulation well worth investigating—like the other childhood memory, later in date, of the lantern maker who claimed to have led the old painter, who had become blind, by the hand when he was little. Where did Vasari get the fable of the father's death? And if it is his own invention, to what intention, to what fantasy did this fable answer for him? An intention that was strictly rhetorical, or more simply narrative, fabulist, as Longhi would have it? As skilled as Vasari was at seasoning his biographies with anecdote, was he reduced, in Piero's case, to borrowing from his own stash? Perhaps, but the invention of the father's death, even before the child's birth, was not on the same register as the fable he recounts at the end of his "life" of Piero: that of Lorentino, one of his students, who painted a figure of Saint Martin in exchange for a pig he consumed with his family.[32]

In the matter of lighting, such an "invention" could not but inflect, to some degree, the image that our culture has formed of Piero, or at least of the author of the works attributed to him. And among these the *Madonna del Parto,* whose impact is clearly of a piece with the image's own connection to the oldest and most burning question of young humanity: a question in effect so virulent, even on the level of reception, that, just looking at the fresco in the silence of the chapel in Monterchi (as one could still do until recently), visitors were prone to ruminate on a past that must be called generic: the human species, unlike the animal kingdom generally, recognizing itself in, among other things, the riddle or mystery that generation represents for it, as much as the sexual difference from which it proceeds. And "representation" is not saying too much in this instance, for if the *Madonna del Parto* awakens such echoes in the spectator, whoever he or she might be, it is not only because the Virgin exhibits her rounded belly. As Freud goes on to note, "that the baby grows inside the mother's body is obviously not a sufficient explanation."[33] Such was the genius of the painter to whom we are indebted for the fresco in Monterchi that he managed, through his art, to give iconic (or should we say ideogrammatic?) force to an enigma that the Christian mystery itself encompasses but incompletely. By what paths, in what form, with what effects (effects that are discernible in the fresco itself), this is what we shall see farther on. But the fact that he succeeded in this is sufficient indication that this mystery resonated in all the individuals who participated in the same culture, as it does even today in tourists who travel to Monterchi, with a very archaic memory, bearing the stamp of primary theories, those of early childhood: a time—Freud writes further—when "the infantile sexual components could find expression in theories in an uninhibited and unmodified fashion."[34] As they occasionally do in painting, however pure and elaborated, however "adult" it might be.

3

"However widely children's later reactions to the satisfaction of their sexual curiosity may vary," wrote Freud, "we may assume that in the first years of childhood their attitude was absolutely uniform, and we may feel certain that at that time all of them tried most eagerly to discover what it was that their parents did with each other so as to produce babies."[1] Historians and anthropologists will be tempted to object that it is a bit hasty, on Freud's part, to ascribe absolute universality to something that we have reason to think was and is prone to different modulations in time as in space, given that many so-called archaic peoples do not establish a necessary connection between copulation and generation.[2] And this, quite apart from the fact that when it comes to past centuries we can know childhood behavior only indirectly, by way of its traces and echoes in remarks, writings, and works dating from adulthood.

As regards Piero's contemporaries, we at least know that they gave the greatest attention to kinship relations (as evidenced by the *ricordanze,* or "family books," in which Florentines who could wield a pen recorded the events and expenditures of everyday life), going so far as to see in the facts of descent and lineage, and in the genealogies they diligently traced, the surest guarantee of the identity of a "house" and its constituent individuals.[3] Which is to say that sexual difference was the most constant horizon of the work that took place in the secrecy of the scrittoio (as was the case for perspective with Paolo Uccello), women, although having their say in the business, being as a general rule kept some distance from this eminently masculine activity. But women, like moveable objects and a medium of exchange, were always only passing through the "houses" where men, inversely, had their roots, and in this respect represented, as Klapisch-Zuber aptly put it, "a ferment of instability, an insistent grating in the whir of the genealogical cogwheels, in sum, a menace to peace and to masculine integrity."[4] In this context, the Christian mystery of the child miraculously born of a Virgin—the "legal" father being, if not ousted, then at least relegated to an ambiguous position—could not help but resonate, on the one hand, with the problem of generation and of the respective roles of the two sexes in its process, such as this was formulated at the time in terms one hesitates to call scientific; and on the other hand, with the buried memory of an archaic questioning of the enigmas of sexual life dating back to earliest childhood, whatever form it might have assumed, at a time when adult speculation often directly echoed it.

In this context, the fact that the *Madonna del Parto* took its place in the territory of the maternal family, in the proximity of Borgo, should be considered in tandem with the strong local implantation of Piero's oeuvre, in the very place where the paternal lineage had its roots and where the painter chose to make his domicile so as to return there regularly until his death, and ultimately to be buried there. So it goes too with the question of the name, often considered trivial but in fact a decisive link, on the level of the signifier, between the collective and individual registers, as well as between what might pass for "objective" and what would pertain to subjectivity. As Klapisch-Zuber has shown, the name, or more precisely the system of family names and given names, was one of the most effective supports of male identity at the time. Now it isn't a stretch to proceed likewise in the field which is that of the history of art. Of the "author" discernible behind the works attributed to him with greater or lesser certainty, this discipline often has retained only the name, which it places in the foreground largely for taxonomic reasons, while scholars track it in the archives in hopes of finding in it, as much as proofs or indices, the traces of an activity, the outline of a role. And this, without taking into account the fact that it is hard to see what, in his writings, apart from the author's very name, might make it possible to go a bit farther in knowledge of "the man Piero," in accordance with Freud's project as regards "the man Leonardo" and "the man Moses"—if it was not already Vasari's, in terms that were radically different, to be sure, but prone nonetheless to an analogous drifting off course.

The author of the *Lives of the Painters* indeed had some good reasons to take seriously the problem posed by the feminine first name given at baptism, which in this case follows an initial first name: Piero (or Pietro, since that is how he is usually designated in the documents) *della Francesca*. The fable holding that Piero was baptized "after the name of his mother, because she had been left pregnant with him at the death of her husband, his father, and because it was she who had brought him up and helped him attain the rank that his good fortune held out to him" is not, as Longhi maintains, just a rhetorical invention with which Vasari sought, from the outset, to enliven a narrative by no means teeming with anecdotes, the documents attesting only to facts about commissions, family or community affairs, and the late payment of a tax.[5] Another fiscal document, published in 1916 by Alessandro della Vita, was at the origin of what is regarded as Vasari's "misunderstanding": in the *catasti*, or tax registers, of the commune of Arezzo, Piero's brother Antonio, after having been inscribed in 1490, as a property owner, under the name "Antonio della Francesca," was inscribed from 1493 until 1544, obviously due to an erroneous transcription, under that of "Antonio di m.a. Francesca."[6] Vasari might have had knowledge of this fact: the fable (or should we say: the novel?) that he saw fit to imagine to justify this denomination, supposing that he was its author, still indicates that such a patronymic did not, at the time, go without saying.

We saw how this fable anticipated in its way the novel that Freud would construct in his own essay on Leonardo da Vinci, from the moment it got down to establishing the young Piero in a situation or position comparable to the one alleged to have been the young Leonardo's—especially since, while Freud presents the latter as the only son of his natural mother, Vasari says nothing about either the brothers or the sisters of Piero. The rapprochement imposes itself all the more forcefully because some authors, not content with repeating Vasari's fable, have claimed that Piero's father remarried, and that Piero, like Leonardo, had not one but two mothers. Even if this were not pure fantasy (it has no basis whatsoever), the problem would remain intact. In the documents, the person Vasari calls, in the last paragraph of the life, "Piero Borghese" is sometimes designated Pietro *di Benedetto,* the second given name being, as was customary, that of the father (the first one belonging to the grandfather), and sometimes Pietro *dei Franceschi* or *della Francesca.* Now the father and grandfather already appear, in documents dating from the period of Piero's birth, under the names de Benedetto and (the late) Pietro della Francesca. Hence *dei Franceschi* has every appearance of being a given name turned into an hereditary name, in short a patronymic, which was in principle a privilege of the dominant class but whose usage was then becoming more widespread. To be sure, Borgo was not Florence, and there was nothing aristocratic about Piero's family; but commerce in leather as in wool, and the ownership of property, urban and rural, sufficed to guarantee it, at least locally, an enviable position. If it is true that the hereditary name, which appears even before the thirteenth century, long remained an indicator of social rank and political responsibility, whereas each individual participated, thanks to his given name (which often repeated that of an ancestor), in this entity that was the lineage, the *casa,* then the testament of 1487 is curious insofar as it combines the two denominations, feminine and singular, masculine and plural, the first being reserved for the painter: "*testamento di Piero della Francesca pittore del fu Benedetto di Pietro di Benedetto dei Franceschi.*"[7]

The name "della Francesca," which appears in many documents concerning the father, Benedetto, as well as his children, and even his nephews, is not simply a feminization of the patronymic, which by the same token would occupy the position of a second given name. For although an individual was then identified by a series of two or three masculine given names, his own followed by the name of his father and then perhaps a third given name, to preclude mistakes about who he was within a given lineage, the rule in Tuscany was that no feminine given names were ever intercalated.[8] For this reason, neither should the feminine form "della Francesca" be confused with the introduction of a name from the maternal stock, a turn whereby a system of naming based essentially on the paternal lineage could subtly adjust indications that were too exclusively agnate to make room for cognate ancestry. Must we see here, with Eugenio Battisti, a usage that was "popular," or, better yet, routine (but that did not apply only to *Pietro pittore*), in the pre-Tridentine period, when the church, which was there to reiterate that parentage in the Christian world was cognate,[9] constantly endeavored to maintain an equal balance between paternal and maternal ancestry, and when it was not considered wrong to femininize the names of apostles and great saints?[10] Or should we see here an indication of a latent conflict between the two parties to the matrimonial alliance, the maternal lineage having managed in this case to assert itself in a way that is, to say the least, unexpected?

In this context, constant passage from the private sphere to the public sphere, and vice versa, is as unavoidable as passage from what presents itself as a conscious elaboration to what would be its hidden mainspring. Klapisch-Zuber has shown that even though those great theorists of the family who were the Florentines of the Renaissance gave considerable thought to the family name that, circumstances permitting, one generation transmitted to another, the choice of given names, by contrast, was an obscure zone of family consciousness.[11] Now it is this same obscure zone that is referenced by the work, in legend as well as doctrine, of Christ's miraculous conception and birth, echoes redounding from the one field to the other, as is confirmed by the art of the Trecento and the Quattrocento. Millard Meiss underscored the new emphasis, in fourteenth-century Tuscan painting, on themes reflective of familial and bourgeois values, from marriage to birth and the education of children.[12] To say nothing of older motifs, often borrowed, through the *Golden Legend,* from a tradition in which the "apocryphal" gospels played an important role. If the gospel of Luke effectively served as the basis for the development of the iconography of the Annunciation, this does not hold for other episodes in the story related to the conception, gestation, and virgin birth of Christ—episodes that would enjoy a considerable vogue in painting: such as the Visitation and above all the Nativity, with all the luxurious settings and tableaux, all the processions and vignettes that the Christmas legend could accommodate.

I will limit myself here to two or three examples of interaction between theology, or perhaps even Marian iconography, and the sphere which could be that (at least relatively speaking) of private life.[13] The

questions posed by men of the Renaissance, in Tuscany, about relations between the sexes within the bosom of the family as well as outside of it, these questions were effectively formulated, through transpo-
sition, in terms analogous to those of the Gospels. And better yet (the
New Testament answering but incompletely to the expectations of the
first Christians, who saw in the virgin birth of Christ not just a sign but
the necessary premise of his divinity), in terms analogous to those of the
apocryphal gospels: part of their immense popular success being due to
the fact that under cover of theological and doctrinal reflections which
nonetheless obeyed very strong mythic constraints, Christian humanity
constantly made up theories that were often quite sophisticated, but that
nonetheless reconnected with a number of archaic fantasies, even as they
awoke multiple echoes in contemporary life.

A first interaction followed from what the gospels present as the
genealogy of Christ. The gospel of Matthew sees no contradiction in
situating the Davidic ancestry of Jesus in the paternal line; Luke, in his
genealogy of Jesus, is keen to underscore that Joseph was only the puta-
tive father.[14] How, then, to conceive (if the reader will allow me this
word) the role or position of the father in terms of filiation, if not of
generation? The Church Fathers solved the problem by making Mary a
cousin of Jesus, herself of the house of David, which amounted to oust-
ing the father a second time, on the genetic plane as well as the social. If
we can believe Marina Warner (who adduces the work of Edmund Leach
by way of support), concern with proving Jesus' ancestry and by the same
token his authenticity took precedence, when Matthew and Luke were
writing and for the audience they addressed, over the urgency of arguments in favor of the virgin birth. It was all very well for Matthew to
view this birth as a symbol that conferred legitimacy on Jesus as God; it
was still incompatible with his legitimacy as a social being with a socially
acknowledged father. In a patriarchal society, even the Messiah could be
legitimate, socially speaking, only if his mother were properly married.[15]

What has been called the "patrilinear paradox" is most strikingly
illustrated in the genealogical charts and family origin narratives from
which women and relations by marriage were excluded. The paradox
being most acute in the case of a generation considered miraculous, and
from which the titular father was excluded, not without resistance on his

part. Here again, the argument used to justify Mary's virginity after her marriage to Joseph accorded with Quattrocento matrimonial practice. If Mary could ask the angel the question that Luke ascribes to her ("But how can this come about, since I am a virgin?"; Luke 1:34), this, it bears repeating, was because Jews married only after a long period of betrothal during which the woman was already considered the man's legal spouse, according to the terms of a contract that could not be voided, carnal consummation taking place only after celebration of the nuptial rites. Now the same seems to have held, at least in principle, in Florence, in the fourteenth century and at the beginning of the fifteenth, the woman being obliged first to be "betrothed," then "married" (or "ringed"), and finally "brought" to her husband, led under his roof: there being a clearly marked temporal gap between the contractual phase that regulated the woman's transfer from one group to another, and the festive, highly ritualized phase that organized her physical transfer to her husband's house. This encounter between two sets of practices, and the solution it provided to an especially prickly point of dogma, explain, at least in part, the fortune in Italian art after Giotto of the theme of the *spozalizio,* or marriage of the Virgin. But the rules were sometimes contravened: for many reasons, not all of them libidinal in nature, the delay between the *matrimonium* and its carnal consummation was constantly growing shorter, to the great consternation of moralists and men of the Church,[16] rekindling by the same token—or so it might be supposed—a questioning, which in fact never would have ceased, that bore on a history which served as both model and foil for contemporary practice in the matter of sexuality.

Insofar as they could be conceptualized in terms of law or custom, the legitimacy of the child, even the virginity of the mother, was one thing, its filiation another. In the oldest commentary on the New Testament, namely the Epistle to the Romans, Saint Paul has this pithy formulation, which simultaneously opens and sums up the debate: "This news is about the Son of God who, according to the human nature he took, was a descendant of David: it is about Jesus Christ our Lord who, in the order of the spirit, the spirit of holiness that was in him, was proclaimed Son of God in all his power through his resurrection from the dead" (Romans 1:3–4). But the idea of the double nature of Christ, at once human and divine, was more or less explicitly suggested as early as the first gospels, with all the ensuing doctrinal problems and all the possibilities for drifting off course, to the point of heresy. Taken literally, the formulation from the Epistle to the Romans (which in its way serves as a genealogy) maintains that the child "born of a woman," as Paul further writes in the Epistle to the Galatians (4:4), was born man, and that this man was elevated to divine standing by the effect of his Resurrection, before time, from the dead. Which was very much in the spirit of the evangelism of Paul, for whom the Resurrection was the great mystery at the same time as a constant obsession—as it would be for the first Christians and for the early Church, which continued to view the Resurrection as the touchstone of salvation. But another theme would soon take hold of Christian consciousness: that of the virgin birth of Christ and of the virginity of the Virgin, *virgo intacta post partum,* which would give rise to a doctrinal work that was, to say the least, intense.

The notion of virgin birth as a sign of divinity had been present in Jewish culture: the prophecy of Isaiah invoked in the gospel of Matthew, through the voice of the angel who appears to Joseph in a dream to dissuade him from repudiating Mary, indicates this explicitly: "the maiden is with child and will soon give birth to a son whom she will call Immanuel" (Isaiah 7:14). If, as Marina Warner maintains, myth played a certain role in shaping the text of Matthew, a constraint of another order was responsible for imposing the idea of divine paternity as the necessary condition of the virgin birth and of the divinity of Christ. The same one that, in the *Book of James* and all the apocryphal books deriving from it, displaced the gospels' emphasis on the divinity of the adult Christ onto the miracle of his arrival on earth.[17] This resulted in the Virgin coming to the fore, and with her an imagery whose agreeable, reassuring tenor made it quite different from the dark scenes of the Passion and the Last Judgment.

The canonical gospels give only limited space to Mary, who furthermore is not always presented there in the most favorable light.[18] The account of the childhood of Christ in the gospel of Luke is nonetheless the preeminent source of the great "mysteries" associated with the figure of the Virgin, if not with her person. Of the four dogmas of the divine Maternity, post partum virginity, the Immaculate Conception, and the

Assumption, only the first one derives unequivocally from the gospel of Matthew, as well as from Luke. But this was enough to appeal to the imagination that is described a bit hastily as "popular," for the Fathers and theologians of the Church, not to be outdone, did better and more than satisfy the expectations of their readers. And how could it have been otherwise, given that the problems they were dealing with were directly connected to what Freud called the oldest and most burning question of young humanity?

A similar work of thought seems to justify the functional analogy noted by Freud between the genesis of childhood memories and the birth of what he calls the writing of history (*die Geschichtsschreibung*) among ancient peoples: in both cases, we are dealing with constructions that answer to a need to know where we come from and how we come to be (*woher man gekommen war und wie man geworden war*). Constructions, in written history, that mobilize a set of traditions, legends, and survivals to constitute something like a history of archaic times (*eine Geschichte der Vorzeit*), but that do not so much reflect the past of the peoples in question as express their present views and desires. "A man's conscious memory of the events of his maturity is in every way comparable to the first kind of historical writing [a chronicle of current events]; while the memories that he has of his childhood correspond, as far as their origins and reliability are concerned, to the history of a nation's earliest days (*die Urzeit*), which was compiled later and for tendentious reasons."[19]

Now it is indeed, if not to the prehistory of Christianity (the old law), then at least to the *Urzeit* of the New Covenant that the *Madonna del Parto* implicitly alludes. Or, to put it differently, and to avoid appealing at the outset to what would be, in iconographic terms, its "subject" (the one it allegedly "represents," a question that Freud himself would pose explicitly, some years after his essay on Leonardo, with regard to Michelangelo's *Moses*), it gestures or points toward this Urzeit by designating, if not the site of a conception whose paths, as we know, have always been problematic, then at least that of gestation and parturition. Doubtless Christianity has not been the only religion in history to conflate the moment of its origin with that of a miraculous birth. The Old Testament had set the tone. But the question "Where do children come from?" nonetheless took a singular turn in Christian theology, lending itself to all kinds of fantasies and constructions every bit as singular and bold as childhood sexual theories can be in the moment, as Freud writes, when early childhood sexuality expresses itself without inhibition and without transformation. Constructions (fantasies) that not only channeled themselves through speech and writing but likewise managed to become manifest, to *produce themselves,* in figurative guise: if I spoke of ideograms in connection with the *Madonna del Parto,* this was the better to emphasize the link between the work of historical writing such as went on even in the retreat of the scrittoio, and the work perhaps carried out by art in the analogously remote place where the *Madonna del Parto* was situated, even if the construction from which the latter springs (and whose artifice is sufficient justification of the aforementioned analogy with a childhood memory) aimed, as we shall see, at something like a suspension of the narration, if not a blockage of the story to which all history—and "Sacred" History first of all—comes down in the last analysis.

At this point another analogy presents itself, one between the questioning of history and that of works of art. Those same works about which Walter Benjamin boldly wrote that "the entire sphere of their life and effects have just as many rights, indeed even more, as the history of their composition"—so much so that the problem is less to deal with works in relation to their time than "to bring to representation [*zur Darstellung zu bringen*] the time that perceives them—which is our own—in the time that brought them forth"[21]: the question as to where works of art come from and how they are born eliciting in its turn modes of investigation doubtless quite different from those that bear on generation and filiation, but that nonetheless lead to many constructions in which the work of fantasy is often discernible. And this, all the more surely insofar as the latter are allegedly based only on "facts." Where do children come from? Where do works of art come from? Doubtless the two orders of problems are not to be conflated, but neither are they unconnected on the level of the imaginary.

This is as much as to say that the idea of discussing Piero's *Madonna del Parto* under the heading "childhood memory" entails a project very different from the one that was Freud's in his *Leonardo,* despite the fact that it will echo this and reflect its basic articulations.

In plain language, all "application" of psychoanalytic principles and methods to the "Piero case," in view of "taking hold" of the domain of biography—Freud's hope—is excluded from the outset. I repeat: we know nothing about Piero's childhood and very little about his adult life, apart from what we learn about it from the fable of the father's having died before the child's birth, to say nothing of the one of the blind old painter having been led through the streets of Borgo by another child. But these fables nonetheless have symptomatic value insofar as they correspond to constructions that answer in part, intentionally or otherwise, the question that I posed at the beginning of this essay, taking Freud's *Leonardo* as my model. For the problem indeed lies here, and touches on the very idea of "birth": with the result that the mystery attached to the birth of a work of art metaphorically doubles that of the birth of its author. Such a rapprochement gives us warrant to take as one pole of our inquiry not a childhood memory as such but the very idea or notion of *construction* that implicitly subtends, in Freud's text, the concept of "childhood memory," in order to compare it with an artifice that, although different in nature, is nonetheless well characterized, and is itself connected to the question of such interest to humanity, whether young or adult. And this without there being a need for us to reference, at any moment of the analysis, "the man Piero," save in a purely abstract and nominal way. But without for all that our being prohibited from appealing, when need be, to certain traits that might have played a role in the genesis of the said fables—which themselves pertain to another way of writing history—touching on, if not "the man Piero," then at least his identity. Beginning with his name, and with the works that give this name some semblance of the thickness or relief, be it purely taxonomic, of a "personality."

That Marian theology and iconography was able to reconnect
with, without being reduced to, a more or less repressed and fantasy-
based archaic questioning, and to the point of awakening, reactivating,
even renewing it by providing it with an outlet, so much is self-evident:
something perhaps not in the best taste to point out, but that has nothing to do with the appeals to folklore and pagan tradition embraced by
many interpreters.[1] What it is important to grasp, if the analytic angle
of the metaphor of the childhood memory is to prove pertinent here,
seeing as we're dealing with the *Madonna del Parto,* is the way Sacred
History as well as traditional imagery could have provided the painter
with the material, or better yet a point of departure, even an indispens-
able pretext, for a work of symbolization that could be summed up as
a successful construction of, and conjunction with, the interests of the
"young humanity" dear to Freud. André Gide (in a passage quoted in
the definition of *appropriation* in the *Petit Robert*) esteemed that "what
makes a masterpiece is a mutual suitability or happy match between subject and author." But what makes Piero's fresco the slightly incongruous masterpiece that consensus takes it to be is not just this coupling
effect, whereby the treatment of its theme or "subject" imposes in turn
the idea of an "author": an artist to whom, whatever some might say,
it cannot have been a matter of indifference that he was painting this

image of maternity on the outskirts of the town where his mother was born, although no conclusions can be drawn from this about the work itself. Another fact should also be taken into account, one directly linked to the emergence, the surging forth of the said "subject," in both senses of the word: a surging forth, in the painted image, of what is to be its subject (to put it differently, but less well: its "matter" or "content"); but a surging forth too, concomitantly, of the subject in the philosophical and analytic senses, due to constraints imposed both by the question that traverses the painting and by the latter's figuration of this. The very term *subject* first summoning up the idea of a dependence, a *subjugation*, before invoking, through a characteristic reversal, and by way of the grammatical subject, a being that is autonomous and in control of itself, master of its actions: in other words, a figure, in this respect, and as an effect of the construction occasioned by it, not without analogy, at least functionally, to a childhood memory.

If the history of art, usually so partial to biographical allusions, refuses in this instance to take into account the location of the *Madonna del Parto* in the territory of the maternal lineage, this benefits interests that must be called more high-minded. In terms of symbolization, the problem is less one of determining what this work might imply about its author in the way of personal investment, or even what it "represents" from a strictly iconographic point of view (one characterized aptly enough by its customary title), than one of extracting its deep meaning insofar as this can be translated into words, in conformity with the program of iconology: the emphasis regularly being placed on the work's "signified," which it is up to the interpreter to decipher by using all the resources at his disposal so as, in accordance with the wish that was Aby Warburg's in his time, to assign a meaning to images, and first of all to make them speak (which too often amounts to torturing them). Hence, since we're dealing with a sacred image, the obligatory references to the biblical text and to the exegetical tradition as well as to the theology, Marian in this instance, which supposedly provide the words and syntagms, if not the propositions, that are lacking in the fresco but nonetheless correspond to the linguistic framework within which it would have been expected to work. Without neglecting the many channels whereby Christian dogma could be transmitted to the faithful—beginning with painters and their patrons—depending on their cultural level, through liturgy, ritual, and various forms of religious practice as well as through devotional literature and even preaching, doubtless the decisive factors here—as father Giovanni Pozzi rightly insists in what is to this day, despite its doctrinal and epistemological limitations, the most fully elaborated and most rigorous discussion of the iconology of the *Madonna del Parto*. Not to mention the special reverence that the inhabitants of Monterchi, beginning with its women, always felt for an image that, until its ill-advised recent displacement, remained *in situ*, despite the presence there of avatars who oversaw the gradual reduction of the church of the Momentana to a small chapel without character, and a change of orientation ultimately imposed on the fresco—and this notwithstanding the fact that the feast of the *Expectatio B. M. Virginis* (December 18), introduced by the Franciscans in 1263 and extended throughout Christendom by Urban VI in 1389, adduced by Battisti in connection with the *Madonna del Parto*, does not seem to have been celebrated in central Italy in Piero's day.[2]

Giovanni Pozzi rightly notes that the destiny of a work of art is not limited to its critical fortune. But if the devout of both sexes, in their prayers, can associate with it traits or elements alien to what is, from a strictly iconographic point of view, its "signified," and if piety (as Pozzi also says, despite his attentiveness to iconological as well as religious dogma) does not necessarily respect "iconographic modules," these avatars belong, here again, to what Walter Benjamin, discussing works of art, called "the entire sphere of their life and effects." A sphere, as we said, to which he ceded as many rights (if not more) as he did to the history of their "birth," the only one iconology wants to know about, including the one that is the very matter of the present work: a history, precisely, of "birth," and one that, as such, is far from self-evident. To try, as Pozzi does, to establish a hard and fast line between the specific object of iconology and what pertains to a history of piety amounts, whatever his intentions, to removing the work of painting from history so as to discuss it in terms of a dogmatics, all the while feigning ignorance of the fact that iconological practice, like devotional practice, pertains to a history of reception. The only discrepancy between the two being iconology's pretension to a kind of "truth" that will suffer no deviation.

Unlike Maurizio Calvesi, who flatters himself that he has uncovered the "true meaning" of the *Madonna del Parto*[3] (as if the "meaning" of art were a matter of true or false), Pozzi does not abuse this notion, and limits himself to discussing the symbolic in terms of metaphor, under the double rubric of "comparing" and "the compared." This gives him warrant to elide, like Calvesi, the question of the *signified,* despite the fact that nothing else is in question in either case. Both Pozzi and Calvesi connect the image of this woman, obviously pregnant and standing under a dais in the form of a pavilion (from the Latin *pavilio,* "butterfly") whose two flaps (or wings) are held open by two symmetrically disposed angels, with the configuration described in chapters 25 and 26 of Exodus, the model for which was allegedly given to Moses by Yahweh: namely the tabernacle, which was sheltered by a tent made of sheets of goat hair covered with ram skins and fine leather (Exodus 26:14), and within which was enclosed the Ark of the Covenant. Ignoring the set of associations (based according to him on approximate readings of erroneous references) that led Calvesi to see in the Virgin an analogue simultaneously of the tabernacle and the ark, surmounted as the latter was by a throne of mercy at the two ends of which were cherubim made of gold, their wings spread (Exodus 25:18–29), as well as the many references to the tabernacle of Exodus scattered through the text of Jerome's Latin translation of the Bible, Pozzi chose to rely, rightly it would seem, only on the three verses of the Vulgate that have some bearing on Marian exegesis: first, the description in Exodus of the mobile tent set up by the Hebrews in the desert (Exodus 25–26); and second, verse 5 of Psalm 45 of the Vulgate ("*sanctificavit tabernaculum suum altissimus*"), often invoked in Piero's day with regard to the Immaculate Conception and the sojourn of the Word in the womb of Mary, this latter being, by contrast, the only theme of the allegory drawn by Marian exegesis from the third text adduced by Pozzi, which he takes from Ecclesiastes (24:9–12), still in the version of the Vulgate ("*Qui creavit me requievit in tabernaculo meo*").[4] As he does in order to get—if I may say—to the bottom of things, the "subject" of the *Madonna del Parto,* Pozzi adhering strictly to the formula held out by the devotional literature, which he thinks the most accurate translation of the "message": that is, something between the "*corpus Mariae quasi tabernaculum,*" drawn from the commentaries on the Psalms by the pseudo-Jerome, the "*tabernaculum Filii Dei,*" which accords with the dogma of Mary *theotokos,* "mother of God," and the

"*Verbum infans,*" the Word made flesh—the word *in-fans,* the word that does not have (or no longer has) speech, the word made image—which confirms it. In such a way that the *Madonna del Parto* would be nothing other than a translation into figurative terms of the mystery of the Incarnation, the denomination "Mary-tabernacle" fitting the icon as nicely as a tracing: "The act of Piero which associates the tabernacle to gravidity is analogous to that of the exegete or preacher who says '*per tabernaculum significatur Maria.*' Which gives us warrant to recognize in the work of the painter the same givens that verbal tradition had elaborated while playing on this metaphor. All these givens, and nothing else."[5]

The configuration conceived by Piero doubtless justifies the reference to the tabernacle of the Old Testament. But it is already going too far to invoke, as Father Pozzi implicitly does, the denunciation by the Council of Ephesus of the Nestorian heresy, which pretended to distinguish between the two persons of Christ, the one human and the other divine, born of the union with the Word.[6] The denomination "Mother of God" suffices to characterize the mystery to which Piero's fresco refers, and about which the faithful were informed without necessarily being able to assess its theological implications—as it suffices to introduce a reflection, albeit elementary, about the status of sacred imagery. As Pozzi recalls, word and image correspond to basic articles of Christian doctrine, the Incarnation of the Word constituting the theological foundation that confers legitimacy upon the image in relation to speech [*parole*]. Just as God created man in his image, the invisible makes itself seen in the flesh. But the question of figurability takes on singular relief in this context, through the detour of a Marian formulation that Pozzi cites: if Christ could not be represented in art, this would mean that he had been born only of the Father and not of the mother: *if the mother is figurable, then the son should be.*[7] The formulation lending itself to a resolutely "modern" reversal, the one effected by Jean-Luc Godard by way of prelude to his film *Je vous salue Marie*: And what if the mother gave herself to vision only through the detour of this body, of this birth *that she received?*[8] Which reconnects with the link noted by Balzac, in "Le Chef-d'oeuvre inconnu," between the impossibility of painting woman and the general question of figurability in the field which is that of art: the Virgin—and, in what would be her "history," the moment of expectancy, when the body of the child has not yet seen light of day—constituting from this point of view, as Dominique Paini has aptly noted, precisely with regard to Godard and his film, *the* subject par excellence.[9]

Whatever the theological or devotional connotations that might become attached to it, the *Madonna del Parto* is first of all what its customary title says it is: the Virgin of childbirth, of parturition. If there is a mystery here, perhaps even *the* mystery, then the knowledge summoned up by this title, the memory mobilized by this image in a context as strongly marked by Marian devotion as was Quattrocento Italy, gives it a resonance without compare. Added to or superimposed on the human mystery is the Christian mystery; or to put it better, the human mystery is, in the Christian mystery, the object of a "sublation" (in the Hegelian sense) that elevates it and makes it attractive in ways doubtless different from the noble and ethereal ones that it assumes in childish discourse, but that nonetheless reconnect, while taking it to a higher level of expression and symbolization, with the question that Freud held to be "the oldest and most burning one of young humanity." Hence the equivocal power that the Christian mystery has never stopped exercising, even over some minds resistant to all religiosity. Part of the "charm"—should we say "eternal"?—of Piero's fresco coming down, to paraphrase Marx, not so much to its correspondence to an image of a still infantile (if not prenatal) humanity as to the echo that it awakens deep within modern viewers of both sexes, as must have happened with Piero's contemporaries, of a maternal image whose singularity is not just a function of the rarity of the iconographic type to which it ultimately belongs: although the *Madonna del Parto* is not unique of its kind, it nonetheless obeys a principle of figurability for its part without example, yet perfectly suited to a mystery itself without precedent, and from which Christian imagery derives a great deal of its meaning.

Far from summoning up the idea of a son born solely of the Father, and not of the mother, the *Madonna del Parto* amounts to a strictly maternal figure of filiation. Not only was the "legal" father marginalized (as he already was, as a general rule, in images of the Annunciation[10] and, without exception, in those of the Visitation); the Father himself is present here only by implication, *in absentia,* whereas he is very much present, in person, like the dove of the Holy Spirit, in the *Annunciation* in Arezzo by the same Piero. If the presence-to-come of the Son is indicated, for those in the know, by the emphatic bulge of the mother's belly, the place of the Father remains unspecifiable. Not that the Father is here absent from his place; it is rather that a place is lacking for the Father, be he divine or legal, and without any such being attributable to him by default (unless it be maintained that he is everywhere in the guise of the mother, considered as the receptacle of his works). If there is lack here, then we must think of it in terms of its relation to the symbolic phallus, the supposed

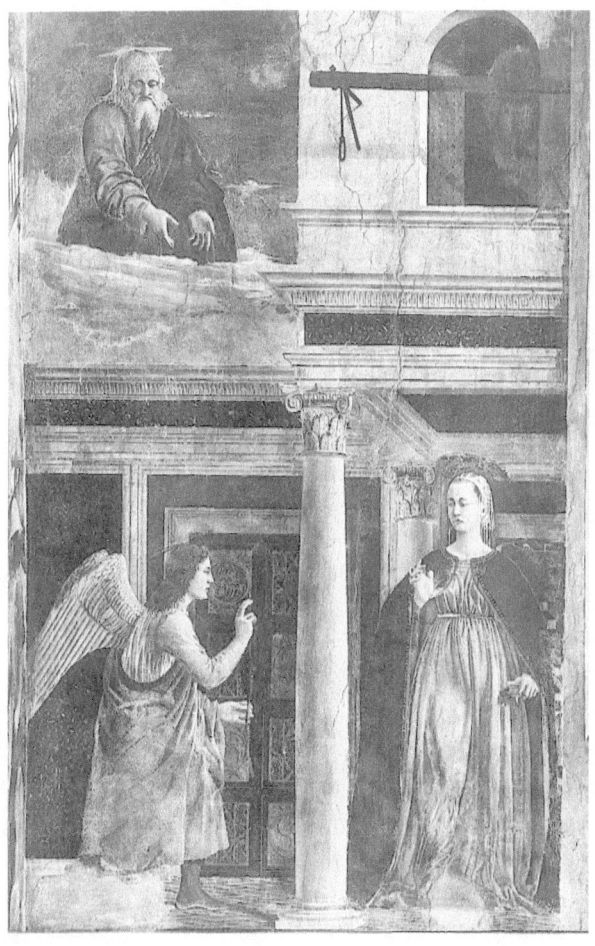

4.1. Piero della Francesca, *The Annunciation*, Arezzo, church of San Francesco.

intervention of the Father being signified in the icon (insofar as it is) only through the detour of the right hand of the Virgin, which simultaneously rests on the vent in her robe and indicates it; and this at the very site corresponding, indissolubly, to the (real) one of childbirth, the (imaginary) one of conception, and the (symbolic) one of castration.

This gesture, which is inflected in a way—I repeat—unprecedented in Christian art, assumes its full meaning only in conjunction with a construction organized in its entirety around this site—or this lack; a construction that, in the state in which the fresco has come down to us, presents itself as being radically *without an outside,* something whose very idea it excludes: at the very least, without an illusionist outside, one articulated as such in the scene, and within its limits. Everything that survives, along the edges of the tent and to either side of its upper part, corresponding to the fall of the flaps, some fragments of blackish background traversed, at the height of the Virgin's head, by what seems to be the beginning of a broad horizontal white band, perhaps part of a decor of faux colored marble—which suffices to refute Baldini's reconstruction of a niche within which Piero would have enclosed the baldaquin. Even if such were the case, the background from which it stood out would still have been completely unrelated to the image of the tent, whose whole configuration turns inward and presents itself as involuted, leaving no room for any "outside-the-field." Beginning with this other gesture, precisely complementary to the posture imparted to the Virgin, left hand perched on her hip and right hand brushing up against the frontal vent of her robe: that of the two angels whose sole office is to hold up the flaps of the tent, like (except for the wings; but only angels have wings) the *velarii* whose function it was, in the residences of wealthy Romans, to lift the curtain at the door for visitors, and whose equivalents are encountered in catacomb paintings and in the mosaics in Ravenna[11]; not to mention the angels who, in the Arena Chapel in Padua, unroll, against a somber red background that seems to be that of the wall, the blue of Giotto's sky.

The gesture of the angels in Padua is a gesture of opening, of unfurling. But what to say about these angels by Piero? Pliny the Elder records a painting by Polygnotus of Thasos in the painted portico of Pompeii in which it is not clear whether the soldier carrying a shield is going up or coming down.[12] Are the angels in the *Madonna del Parto* in the process of opening the tent to reveal the Virgin, or are they by contrast preparing to close it again on this image of triumphant intimacy? The ambiguity of the gesture, if not its suspense, does not preclude seeing it as an act of showing or monstration: as something equivalent, in its authoritarian air, to the biblical *ostentio* or *ostendere* of the tabernacle in Exodus[13]—on condition, yet again, of recognizing there a figure congruent to the posture given the Virgin. The opening (if that's the right word here) being conceptualized less in relation to the exterior than to the vent or fold contrived in the innermost part of the image, and toward which tends everything about the construction that is, as was said, involuted.

Such involution (not to say: such invagination) suggests that the question of the father is posed here, at least implicitly. We know who the child-to-be's mother is; but the father? The one toward whom the scene's whole configuration points would be, of all fathers, the only one—Mary's intact virginity constituting proof of this—certain of being the progenitor of the child carried by the woman, whatever the operative conditions of a conception all the more problematic because a received idea, inherited from Aristotle, had it in the Middle Ages that the man contributed more to the child than did the mother in the process of reproduction[14]: in conception but not in gestation, the latter being a uniquely feminine affair, and centered on the presence, in the symbolic site of lack, of the child to be born. The solitude of the woman here has no equal save

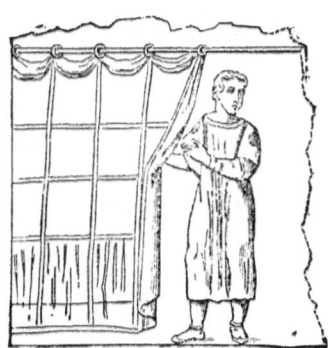

4.2. A *velarius*, from Daremberg and Saglio, *Dictionnaire des antiquités grecques et romaines*, 5 vols. (Paris: Hachette, 1877–1919), vol. 5, p. 675.

for that of the "Virgin of humility," seated on a cushion, directly on the ground or on a carpet of herbs and flowers, in her enclosed garden, in conformity with a Florentine type studied by Millard Meiss.[15] But the Virgin of Monterchi, however alone she might be (the two angels, despite their seeming authority, being of no account, reduced as they are, even in their strict mechanical symmetry, solely to their office as *velarii*), stands upright, not without a hint of pride conveyed by the rotated hand haughtily placed on her hip, and which only makes the bulge of her belly protrude all the more. But above all, she is entitled to this dais in the form of a pavilion that springs from an enclosure analogous to that of the *hortus conclusus* but is otherwise radical and abstract, even conceptual. The painter having somehow managed to push to the limit reflection about the conditions of figurability in the matter of faith and of Marian theology, through the detour of a construction that, rather than playing on the opposition between inside and outside, open and closed, constantly thwarts it: there being no opening here except without an outside, toward an interior in the innermost recess of this body of which nothing is shown, save the very gesture that indicates it.[16]

In its current state, the fresco in Monterchi presents itself as a quasi-experimental configuration in which the icon of the Virgin of childbirth is given to vision without its surroundings, and reduced, in the matter of opening, to the single involution, the single invagination that reaches its apex in the center of the construction (Tarkovsky, in his film *Nostalghia,* having made the mistake of giving the fresco a monumental frame, doubtless because he deemed this worthier of it than the modest chapel in which it was then located). Outside, the night, which would correspond to the few blackish fragments surviving from the mural decor not being handled as in the *Dream of Constantine* of the Arezzo cycle, which likewise takes place in a "pavilion" (another, ancient name for a military campaign tent), certainly cruder but of the same type as the one in Monterchi, and with flaps likewise pulled to either side: Vasari insisting on what he deems the singularly precocious skill with which Piero managed to represent the night into which the scene is plunged, the "pavilion" radiating a light that belongs to it alone,[17] as does the dais below which the Virgin of Monterchi is presented, by contrast with the dark background from which it apparently stood out. But also of the same type, this *padiglione,* as the tent of the tabernacle in Exodus, such as this was represented by Benozzo Gozzoli in the Camposanto in Pisa (the "cherubim" being in this instance replaced by two angels flanking the tabernacle, while the parting of the veil with which it was covered echoes that of the flaps of the tent), and as we encounter it in several carved or enameled Eucharistic tabernacles of the Florentine Quattrocento.[18]

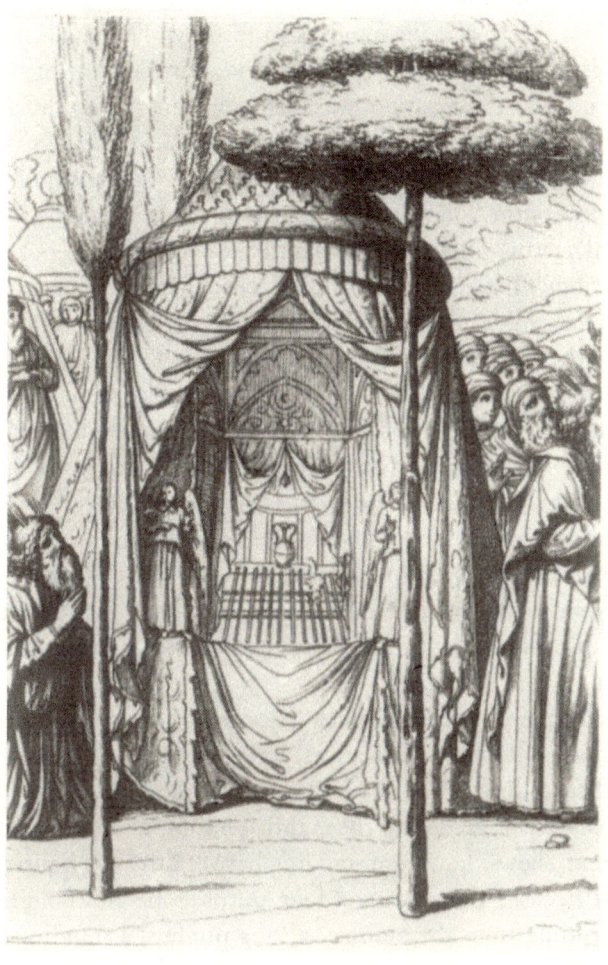

4.3. Benozzo Gozzoli, the tabernacle in Exodus, print after a fresco (lost) previously in the Camposanto, Pisa.

So we are fully justified, even by the upholstered lining of the "pavilion" in the *Madonna del Parto,* in seeing here a reference to the "Tent" of Exodus, as well as to the "Abode" that the latter sheltered, made as it was of linen hangings themselves decorated with cherubim: "skillfully worked" according to the biblical text (Exodus 26:1). And this despite the fact that Piero as well as Gozzoli proposed a singularly reduced and simplified version of the design that Yahweh initially handed down to Moses: the Virgin being substituted for the tabernacle in the Monterchi fresco, or standing in for it, while there is no mistaking the reference to the apocryphal gospels according to which Mary, at the time of the Annunciation, was busy spinning purple thread for the veil of the Temple.[19] "Mary-tabernacle," "*habitatio Filii Dei*"[20]: abode, like the tabernacle of Exodus for the Ark of the Covenant, of the "*Verbum infans,*" of the Son who, through his sacrifice, would be the mediator—Paul's term—of a new covenant or testament (*diathèkè*; Hebrews 9:15). But how different, then, this Virgin-tabernacle or Virgin-abode from the Virgins derived from the Byzantine *Platytera* or from representations of the Apocalyptic Woman, on whose belly a child was painted, eventually within a mandorla (hence the name Platytera, which means "flat mandorla") or a nimbus that they exhibited like a monstrance[21]; and even from Virgin-reliquaries that open to reveal an image of the Trinity in the form of a Christ on the cross supported by God the Father, and toward which descends the dove of the Holy Spirit? How different this image of gravidity, whose "naturalism"[22] some commentators see fit to emphasize, from these icons and ritual objects whose symbolism occasionally raised questions for theologians, sometimes to the point of being censured?

Such would not have been the case with the aforementioned Byzantine images and their derivatives: images usually of modest dimensions, whether lead seals, illuminations, or even fresco paintings. A Syriac manuscript predating the eighth century, and often adduced in this context, shows the Virgin standing between the two figures of Solomon and Ecclesia (?), wearing a long purple robe and holding before her, protruding from the bluish oval of a nimbus, a standing figure of the infant Jesus wearing a long white tunic and draped with a yellow mantle. In images of this type, the gesture, one of the ostension, has no meaning unless its direction is outward and toward the front, inversely to that of the involuted configuration specific to the *Madonna del Parto.* Dom Leclercq, who reproduces the same icon in his *Dictionnaire,* has this to say about it: "One asks oneself what sickly imagination could discern here an image of the pregnancy of Mary."[23] The remark was aimed explicitly at the thesis of Luquet, who claimed that images of

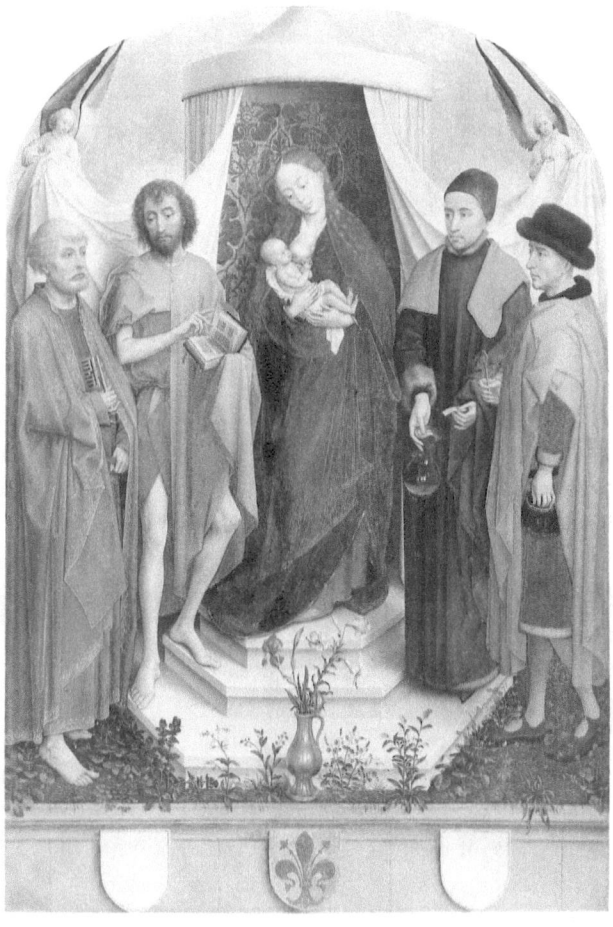

4.4. Rogier van der Weyden, *Virgin and Saints,* Frankfurt-am-Main, Städelsches Kunstinstitut.

this kind exemplified the "intellectual realism" that he believed to be characteristic of the art of children, as well as of that of prehistory and of primitive peoples, by contrast with the "visual realism" specific to classical art: intellectual realism consisting in giving figurative expression to all of an object's constituent elements, even when these are invisible from a set point of view, what Luquet called "representation of pregnancy by transparency" being a limit case insofar as it seemed to him to propose something like a radioscopic image of the gravid body.[24] Although published in the very serious *Revue archéologique,* his analysis is surely not admissible in this caricatural form. Any more than it is applicable to later images in which the figure of the infant is, beyond any "realist" intent, painted directly on the Virgin's robe. But not without the aim having been, here again, all exteriorization or display: in a word, publicity, even propaganda.

However justified, Dom Leclerq's phrase evidences the discomfort that is always incited by any overly direct allusion to the carnal and feminine humanity of the "Mother of God." Now it is precisely this "humanity," if not this femininity, that determined the value of such representations in their day. If nothing gives us warrant to attribute to "the man Piero" a particularly "feminine" sensibility, if not sexuality (devotion for the Virgin being an affair preeminently of the men constituting the priesthood, which derived its dignity from the sacrament signifying that the Son of God is incarnated in their hands by way of the Eucharist, just as had happened in the womb of Mary[25]), this devotion nonetheless accrued, throughout the Middle Ages, a feminine aspect that was ever more pronounced. A prominence accorded by the apocryphal gospels to the childhood of Christ and that of the Virgin in their most domestic aspects that accorded with the notion of a God closer to the humanity he had created in his own image—a humanity, in Caroline Walker Bynum's beautiful expression, rendered "capable of God." And all the more so since God himself had chosen to make himself man, the emphasis on the mystery of the Incarnation serving as prelude to the concentration on the Eucharist in the devotional life of modern Catholicism.

In terms of Incarnation, we should be grateful to father Pozzi for having insisted on the crudity of many of the formulations concerning the divine maternity: "The devotional literature of the time associated the Eucharist with the pregnant Mary with an audacity that would be unthinkable for us, going so far as to speak of the oven of the uterus in which the celestial bread cooked."[26] Even so, representations of Christ's nativity are very far from the realism of many images of

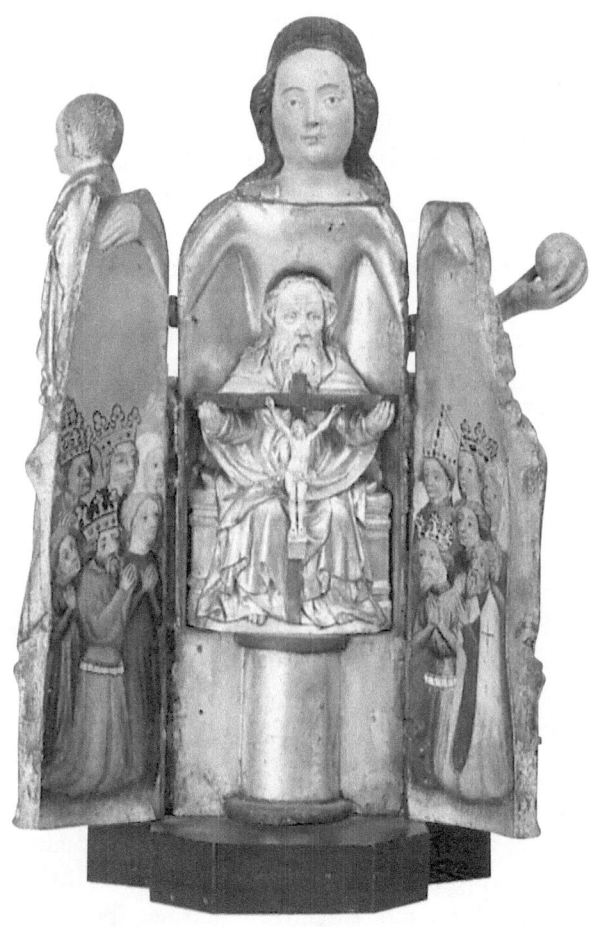

4.5. *Vierge ouvrante*, polychrome wood, eastern Prussia, late fourteenth century, Paris, Musée des Thermes et de l'Hôtel de Cluny.

childbirth found in medieval manuscripts, and not only medical manuscripts. When it came to the birth of the Virgin or that of Saint John the Baptist, imagery at the very least multiplied allusions to specifically material aspects of the event: the baby being washed by servants, the delivered mother remaining in bed and being presented with a fowl cooked *alla matone,* etc. For the infant Jesus, none of this; apart from a few instances when the Virgin is shown reclining near the cradle "like a larvae," in Dom Leclerq's peculiar phrase, the child is represented either as already carefully swaddled or as within a radiant nimbus, the Virgin kneeling close to him in a posture usually less maternal than devout.

If we set aside some more or less harmless figurative jokes—but which, meeting as they did the requirements of figurability, sometimes skirted heresy[27]—touching on the moment of conception, Marian imagery adhered, as regards the Incarnation itself, to an iconography sometimes subtle but also very controlled. There remains the span of pregnancy, on which, however holy it was meant to be, the story (at least in its apocryphal guise) lavished attention. As did iconography; the Visitations and even Annunciations in which the Virgin already seems to be pregnant are proof of this, as are—*a fortiori*—images of *Maria gravida,* a motif that lent itself to iconographic treatment of a traditional type, through the addition to a more or less explicit representation of the Virgin's pregnancy attributes that are apt to underscore its symbolic implications (book resting on the belly, etc.).

Bynum has studied the development in the twelfth century, in Cistercian circles, of an explicitly maternal imagery applied to God and Christ. Already Saint Anselm, even as he criticized the practice of calling God "mother" and argued the superiority of man over woman and the preponderant role of the former in procreation, did not shy away from waxing lyrical about Jesus and Paul as "mothers" of the human soul. Whereas the father governs and produces, the mother loves and nourishes, and first of all gives birth, at risk of her own life. In the twelfth century, Bernard of Clairvaux extended this image to Moses and Peter as well as to priests and abbots, in fact being more attentive to nutrition (breastfeeding) than to conception or gestation. But his followers would not be so discreet; we saw earlier the extent to which an abbot such as Guerric could be fascinated by images of pregnancy, the uterus, and the bowels.[28]

This quite singular imagery went hand in hand with the idea of a God as tender and accessible as a mother. But it did not extend as far as the secondary role that the Aristotelian tradition ascribed to the woman in the process of procreation, which was inconsistent with the idea of the Incarnation (the man gives spirit, life; the woman provides the material, the flesh). Through a symmetrical reversal of what led to the ascription of specifically feminine traits to God, the Virgin came quite naturally to assume, while awaiting her imminent maternity, a phallic character. An astonishing image now in Ferrara, which Longhi identified as the upper portion of *The Dormition of the Virgin* by Mantegna, shows a seated Christ holding in his lap a small figure of the Virgin (or her "soul"?) erect like a phallus, a reversed version of a mother and child.[29] But Piero himself was not loathe to bank on the image of the phallic mother. By contrast with the pavilion in which the *Dream of Constantine* takes place, the tent that encloses the *Madonna del Parto* has no central pole: as if the *entasis* that manifests itself—like the "columnar people" and "columnar humanity" in Longhi's discussion of Piero's figures, to say nothing of the "vermilion trunk"[30] of the *Madonna della Misericordia*—in this allegedly intact body sufficed to establish it in the position of a support, at the same time as the pivot of a construction wholly premised on the retention, at the very site of castration, of an eminently carnal substitute for the paternal phallus—or should we say: for its symbolic equivalent?

An image that is all opening, to the point of excluding the very
notion of an "outside"; a figure turned in on itself as if involuted, opening onto nothing but its own interior, like a reliquary or, in a wholly
different context, certain Indian masks from the coast of the Northwest Pacific coast, themselves known as "opening" or "transformation"
masks, consisting of two interlocking animal faces, those of a bird
and a mammal: it is hard to see, at first glance, how the constructive
turn from which springs, in Monterchi, the image of the *Madonna
del Parto* could accord with Piero's idea of painters' perspective, which
he was the first to treat in strictly geometrical terms. Save by claim-
ing that this construction signals toward the site of lack in the very
way the perspective configuration is organized around what would be
its vanishing point: the confluence—by no means fortuitous, as we
shall see—of the painting's artifice and the limit or "term" to which
Piero maintained *Perspectiva artificialis* was constrained resulting in
an intensification of its effect, as the object intensifies the effect of the
lack that it is supposed to fill.

In the matter of "opening," we are fond of the idea, alleged to date
from Alberti and his treatise on painting, that a painted picture [*tableau*]
is like a window open to the outside world, through which one looks at
what is painted there.[1] Is the *Madonna del Parto* a "picture" in this sense?

The fact that we cannot decide, with any degree of certainty, whether the two angels are lifting the flaps of the tent or are instead closing them suffices to introduce the question: an effect of their gesture's undecidability being that the figure exhibits itself within an interval forever frozen in indefinite suspense, and within the embrasure of something that is in fact neither a window nor a door but rather the entry of a dais-like tent under which the Virgin-tabernacle simultaneously advances and withdraws, at the same time indicating or designating the fold of her robe, as if the better to signify that ultimately it is through here that it passes and must pass.

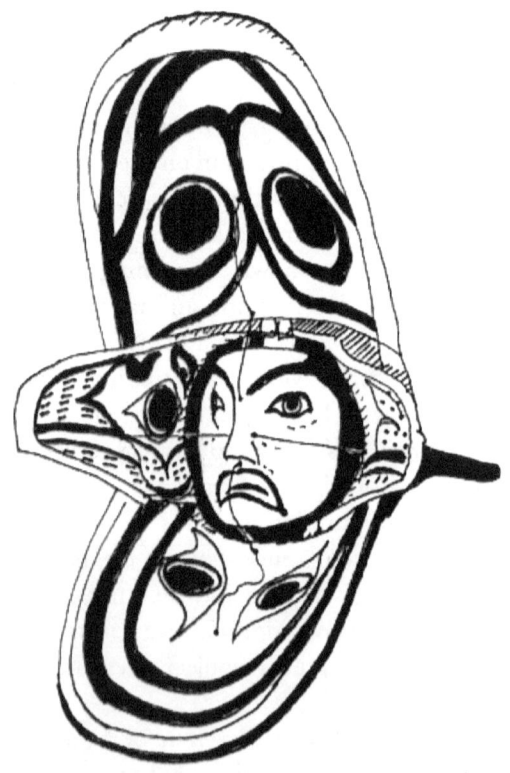

5.1. *Transformation Mask* from the Pacific Northwest (Kwakiutl), New York, Museum of Natural History.

The window metaphor, far from having been invented by Alberti, was taken by him from the ancients. From Pliny on, Latin literature offers many descriptions of rooms decorated with frescoes and paintings resembling so many windows or openings giving onto the surrounding landscape. The antiquity of the topos certainly does not suffice to justify it, any more than to invalidate it. The problem is rather one of knowing what meaning accrues to it and what pertinence this might have to the argument of the first book, ostensibly *tutto mathematico*, of *Della pittura*. The metaphor intervenes in the text precisely at the point where Alberti, after theoretical preliminaries borrowed from geometry and optics, gets down to discussing perspective construction. But it references, quite obviously, the *optical* model on which this is based in principle: the painting being understood as a section through an imaginary pyramid[2] whose apex is in the eye and whose sides are formed by straight lines extending from this point to the contours of a field corresponding to the given angle of vision. Everything happening "as if this surface which they [painters] color [the Italian version has instead "the surface on which are represented the forms of the things seen"[3]] were so transparent and like glass, that the visual pyramid passed right through it from a certain distance and with a certain position of the centric ray and of the light, established at appropriate points nearby in space." And Alberti adds that

Painters prove this when they move away from what they are painting and stand further back, seeking to find by the light of nature the vertex [the apex] of the pyramid (*la punta e angolo, della pirramide*) from which they know everything can be more correctly viewed. But as it is only a single surface of a panel or a wall (*una sola superficie, o di muro o di tavola*), on which the painter strives to represent many surfaces contained within a single pyramid, it will be necessary for his visual pyramid to be cut at some point, so that the painter by drawing and coloring can express [Latin *ut exprimat*; Italian *esprimiere*] whatever lines and colors that intersection presents. Consequently the viewers of a painted surface [Latin *pictam superficiam*; Italian *una pittura*] appear to be looking at a particular intersection of the pyramid. Therefore, a painting will be the intersection of a visual pyramid at a given distance, with a fixed center and certain positions of lights, represented by art (*artificiose*) with lines and colors on a given surface.[4]

Derived as it was from traditional optics—in other words, *perspectiva naturalis*—this model sufficed to justify the use of the "veil" that Alberti

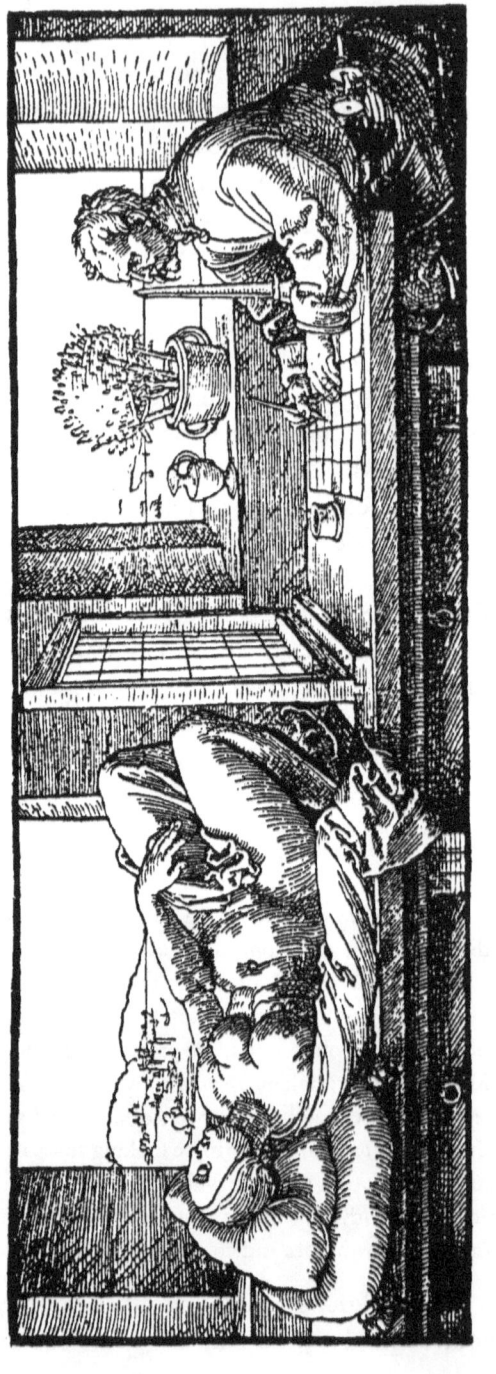

5.2. Albrecht Dürer, *Draftsman Drawing a Nude*, woodcut from *Unterweysung der Messung*, 2nd edition, Nuremberg, 1538.

called the "intersection" and that made it possible according to him to obtain without difficulty, and by means of a so-to-speak mechanical procedure, a perfect tracing of the contours: that is, a fabric made of very thin thread, rather loosely stitched, of any color whatever, divided into squares by thicker threads and stretched over a frame to be placed between the eye and the body or object that one intended to represent, in such fashion that the visual pyramid penetrating the openings in the veil, the contours of the figures, and the limits of the surfaces might easily be transferred to their right and proper place on the panel meant to receive the painting (Latin: *in pingenda tabula*). In fact, this was a strictly mimetic procedure, and one that made it possible to dispense with a wearisome rational construction, nature here seeing itself through, so to speak, at least with regard to figures, as Alberti gives us to understand when, in book three of his treatise, he takes to task those who, copying the works of other masters, fail to understand that their authors strove to represent a figure such as it could be seen painted on the veil by nature (Latin *ab ipsa natura depictum*; Italian *da essa natura dipinto*). This by no means implied that they themselves had resorted to a procedure that the author of *Della pittura* pretended to have been the first to use,[5] by means of a trick that is certainly striking, but whose undeniable practical utility was very far from conferring upon it the exemplary value that many ascribe to it today, something that likewise holds for Dürer's rectangular frame squared with a lattice of string, which springs from an analogous principle.

The veil method, I must emphasize, made it possible to obtain by simple graphic transfer a perfect delineation of the form of things such as they project themselves, draw themselves, "represent themselves" (*si representino*) on a transparent windowpane, as the window metaphor has it. But it could not suffice to construct in a rational way a historical scene or *istoria*, according to Alberti the supreme goal of painting. Hence it is worth underscoring the tension (more than a nuance is at stake here) between the Latin text *De Pictura*, which maintains that painting is like "an open window through which the historia to be painted is seen,"[6] and the version in the vernacular, which holds to the generally accepted idea of a window, itself open, through which one would look at "what would be painted there": the implication being that any pane [*vitrage*] in the window is out of play, outside the circuit. The pane but not the frame, or to put it better the frame or framing of the opening, which in this instance becomes all important. And what does Alberti say when, having finished with what pertains to the *forza del vedere,* the visual pyramid, and the *intersegatione* (in other words, although the concept was formulated only much later, the *plane of projection*), he gets down to describing what he does when he paints: the problem for the painter being not only one of knowing what the section is and what it consists of, but how to generate it, how to produce it: or as Alberti says, "what I do when I am painting."[7] The first operation—the foundational, inaugural gesture—amounting to tracing on the surface to be painted (which might be a wall or panel whose dimensions are larger than the envisaged painting) a rectangle of the desired size, and one that will correspond (it is here that Alberti introduces the metaphor) to the said window. After which the painter will decide how large he wants the human figures in his painting to be (man being, even in art, the measure of all things, and preeminently of history), and will divide this height into thirds, thereby giving it a unit of measure proportional to what the Florentines—"terribly anthropomorphic," in the words of Roberto Longhi[8]—called an arm, *uno braccio,* namely the length of a forearm, between 19.5 and 23.5 inches. Using this module, he will then divide the base of the rectangle that he has first traced into as many such parts as it will hold, and will place a single point where he wishes (*"dove a mi paia,"* but this is an addition in the Italian version), whence he will draw straight lines to each of the divisions on the base line. Alberti called this point "centric" insofar as it was supposed to be an image, as we would say today, on the plane of intersection, of the ray corresponding to the axis of the visual pyramid—but not without intending that this point be placed inside the rectangle, and no higher in relation to the base line than the man that one means to paint there, in such fashion that it will seem to those who look at the picture that they are on the same flat and continuous ground as the objects represented there. The lines drawn from this point toward the divisions on the base line, which corresponded in their turn to the receding lines of a checkered pavement, showing, or better yet, *demonstrating* to the painter (*a mi dimostrino*) how the successive transverse quantities (which correspond to the lines in the checkered pavement parallel to the base line) diminish in accordance with a regular proportion, *usque ad infinitam distantiam,* as the Latin text says, or *quasi persino in infinito,* as we read in the version in the vernacular.

We can interrupt our reading at this point, leaving in suspense the question of infinity such as this is inscribed at the heart of the perspective configuration, on which it confers by the same token all of its speculative import, and ignore what follows: namely, the statement of the principle of construction that will make it possible to determine the placement of

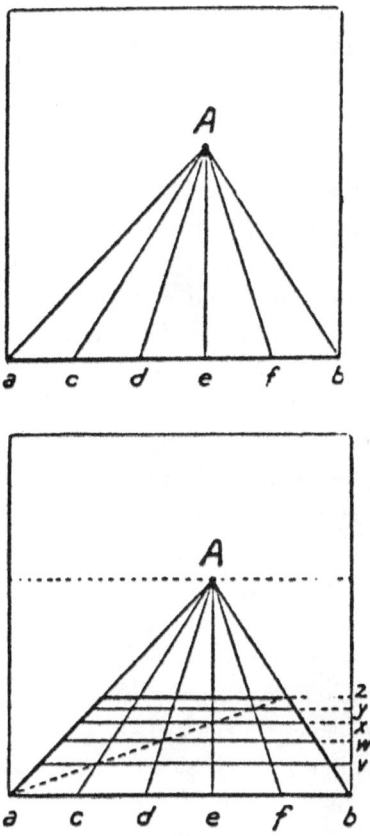

5.3. Schema of the first steps of perspective construction according to Alberti, after Erwin Panofsky.

the transverse lines parallel to the base line of the picture—a problem around which would turn for two centuries, until the conceptual sublation effected under the name of descriptive and projective geometry, all reflection about perspective construction. It will suffice to note that Alberti's statement of the procedure to be followed when constructing the scene on which the *istoria* was called on to take place, or more simply the *site* to be occupied by the things that the painter intended to represent, that this description not only accords ill with the window metaphor but at the limit (I say advisedly: *at the limit*) contradicts it. We saw that the said window opening implied placing the pane outside of the circuit. Does this mean that the metaphor is nonetheless admissible insofar as we adhere to the frame as a given, with its outline corresponding to the institution of the picture as such? The thing seems to go without saying. A window gives onto, has a view of the outside, and the spectacle that it reveals, everything that can be seen through it, is inscribed within limits that are precise but that vary in function with the distance: if I approach it, my field of vision expands; if I back away from it, it gets smaller. Which corresponds, as we would now say, to the language more specifically that of cinema than of photography, and even to the *zoom* to which this lends itself as a kind of *framing*. The term designating nothing other, as Pascal Bonitzer writes, than the partial—in both senses—cutting of reality[9]: a reality about which we must henceforth suppose that it extends behind the wall or surface, beyond the limits of the window, as the receding lines of the picture are supposed to do, the ultimate justification of the metaphor being found in photography, and even more in cinema.

Now it is by no means from a cut of this kind that perspective construction as described by Alberti proceeds, but from a determination (from the Latin *determinare*, "to mark out the limits of") of the field said to be that of the picture insofar as this adheres to the perspective configuration. A field that, from the outset, is strictly defined in its shape (rectangular) and in its limits: its opening in fact merging with its very delimitation, as was already the case in certain classical rituals for the founding of cities. And it is the single given of this delimitation, this originary determination, and this division into equal segments, corresponding to the first row of pavement squares, of the picture's base line (the line, as Alberti assertively writes, "that lies under the rectangle"[10]), that will provide the support or ground, in the strong sense of the word, for the perspective construction. And this without there having been any reference, at any moment, as implied by the window metaphor and the attendant realist bias, to any "outside-the-frame" whatever that might be that of the picture.

This question was not posed explicitly until Piero. Piero who, in his own treatise, gives no place to the window metaphor, any more than to the "veil" method, even though *De prospectiva pingendi* is devoted entirely to that part of painting whose name is *commensuratio*: in other words, to the kind of perspective said to be that of painters (or of painting, in the active, progressive, generative sense of the gerund *pingendi*), as opposed to the "natural perspective" that is the province of traditional, ancient, and medieval optics. But this is precisely because optics plays but a very limited role here, Piero declaring from the start that his concern with vision is limited to the eye, and this only to the extent necessary

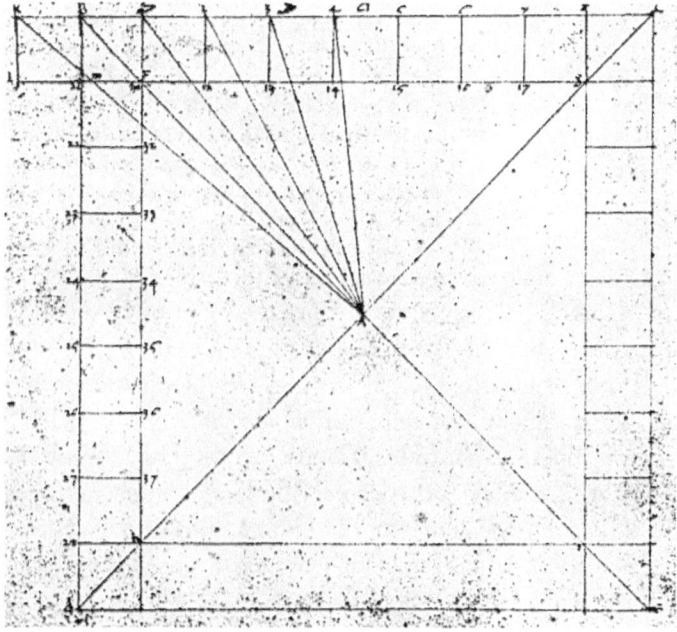

5.4. Piero della Francesca, *De prospectiva pingendi*, fig. 30.

for painting, which follows from one sentence: everything comes from the eye, since it is therein that things seen present themselves at angles varying in function with distance.[11] So it will suffice, to get to the heart of the matter, to give oneself what Piero calls "a term" (*uno termine*) on which the eye will describe things in proportion with its rays, and can judge there of their measure: "Without this term, one could not understand how things get smaller, nor could one demonstrate it."[12]

The "term" in question is of course equivalent to the section through the visual pyramid that Alberti says corresponds to the picture plane. But Piero exploits the way the thing goes without saying precisely to say nothing about it and, by the same token, to dispense with the optical model referenced by the metaphor of the window, as well as with any and all allusion to the "veil" method. It suffices for his argument that one know how to delineate properly anything that one intends to paint there[13]—in other words, how to trace its outlines on the plane. But this argument is of a strictly demonstrative order, *De prospectiva pingendi* presenting itself, as has been said, in its very form, as the first treatise on perspective developed *more geometrico*. Better yet, at least as regards book one, which essentially treats of the construction of the squared pavement to serve as the ground of the perspective scene and as the plane of inscription for the figures (square, triangular, rectangular, hexagonal, and even circular) as well as of the ground plans of the buildings (one square, the other octagonal), themselves "diminished" (*degradate*), to be traced there, the demonstrations are not indebted to anything except plane geometry and the theorems of like figures. Here we have the great novelty of Piero's treatise, precisely from the point of view of a history of science that would take into account the contribution of the arts. But we should not be surprised that it was reserved for a painter to establish that perspective might be a matter of plane geometry, and that starting from points, lines, and surfaces, from figures inscribed on a plane, it might be possible to construct something like a depth. For a painter, and more precisely the author of the Urbino *Flagellation*, about which Longhi would say, admirably, that it was as if depth were seamlessly joined there with positive intervals, and that "the perspective projection displayed the entire scene, bringing to the surface, for the benefit of the eye, a masonry of sumptuous coloristic equivalencies."[14]

The fact that this is one of the secrets of Piero's art suffices to make it henceforth untenable to assimilate the picture plane to a transparent window. But the "mystery" of perspective such as the painter understood it does not end with the result, seemingly paradoxical, that by the grace of painting the (illusionist) depth effect and the (pictorial) surface effect, far from vying with one another, can be mutually reinforcing. It also encompasses how the same picture plane that corresponds, from an optical perspective, to a kind of frame from which the visual pyramid ultimately borrows its form assumes, in the language that is Piero's, its full value as a "term," which is to say, literally, as a *limit*. And this in a double sense, pertaining on the one hand to "the distance there should be between the eye and the *termini* where the things are placed," and on the other to the angle at which the eye apprehends them.

With regard to distance, the thing seems to present no difficulties, although Piero expressly distinguishes between its two guises: on the one hand, the distance of construction, relative simultaneously to the position assigned the point corresponding to the summit of the angle at which things present themselves, in other words to the eye,[15] and to the location of the plane of projection; and on the other hand, the distance from which the painting will ask to be considered, which should not exceed its width, the latter indeed having, in this instance, the value and function of a limit. If we hold to this, if we adhere to this formulation, then the celebrated sentence of Pascal, who thought he could invoke the way that, in the art of painting, a perspective prescribed an indivisible point from which it should be seen, then this metaphor, which is ultimately related to that of the window, simply no longer has any place, at least in the context of the theory as it was articulated in the Quattrocento. But there is another way of understanding it, a way different from optical geometry, whereby the viewer would back away from the picture until he reached a place corresponding to the tip of the pyramid of which the picture is taken to be a section. A way that is specifically perspectival, and a matter, here again, of *opening*.

The first book of *De prospectiva pingendi* ends with a proposition as remarkable in its form as in its content: remarkable in its form, since it amounts to inscribing the eye in the very center of the squared field within which the perspective is called on to operate, as needed for the demonstration. But even more remarkable in its content, since it sets about nothing less than assigning to the perspective construction a limit that could not be more strict, beyond which the construction will lead to aberrations that would raise doubts about its validity. As the chart devised by Piero makes clear, as one moves away from the axis on which the vanishing point is established, the foreshortened squares of the checkerboard will become commensurately elongated until the sides subject to diminution appear to be longer than the divisions on the base line.[16]

So it is a misunderstanding to conflate, as Panofsky does, the "ground" of the perspective construction with the "base plane" of projective geometry, which would extend indefinitely beyond the limits of the picture. A picture constructed in accordance with strict perspective, one consistent with the model adhered to, in theory, by Piero as well as Alberti, and that stipulated that the so-called vanishing point be placed within the *quadro* (which would preclude all oblique perspective): such a picture could not, strictly speaking, be assimilated to a window. To consider it properly, one would have to place oneself, as Pascal required (but for completely different reasons), "neither too close nor too far away": the proper viewing distance not being less, if we are to believe Piero, than half the width of the picture—which corresponds to an angle of vision of less than ninety degrees.[17]

Painting such as Piero understood it was well and truly under constraint, axiomatically, to a limit, or better yet to a *termine,* to use the word employed by him in *De prospectiva pingendi.* Which could not help but affect the economy which was that of representation: for the classic system, and with it the classic scene of representation, insofar as this was governed by the perspective paradigm, rigorously excluded what we would now call an outside-the-frame, save by producing it through the detour, for example, of a mirror supposedly reflecting something situated outside the field of representation, but which is quite obviously captured or caught there, trapped in some way, as with the reflections on the armor of Federico di Montefeltre in the *Brera Altarpiece.* It is against this power simultaneously of exclusion (there is no outside-the-frame) and of captation (there is nothing outside the frame except what is conjured in one way or another within the frame) that the strength of the configuration of classic representation is measured—just as it is against the power that made him inscribe within the two dimensions of a plane the whole coloristic depth of history that even now, despite the ravages of time, we measure the strength of Piero's painting.

In the *Madonna del Parto,* the painter managed to turn to maximal account the constraint which is that of the *termine,* along with the effect whereby every limit logically summons up its own passing-beyond [*dépassement*], its traversal (at the limit), if not its transgression. This construction without any immediately ascribable outside except for the one indicated, at its innermost fold, by the gesture which is that of the Virgin, but that nonetheless summons up, as we shall see, an imaginary beyond through the doubly distorted detour of a perspective that is itself fictive[18] : this construction decidedly has nothing to do with a window such as can be seen in numerous *Annunciations, Nativities,* and *Madonnas and Child,* opening at the back or sides of the perspective cube—beginning with Piero's own admirable *Sinigallia Madonna.* Paradoxically, it is perhaps in the fresco of the *Madonna del Parto* as we see it today, isolated, cut off from its surroundings by something that in fact intervenes like a framing, in the photographic sense of the word, that painting comes closest to the operation which is that of the picture as understood by Piero—just as it comes closest to the artifice which is that of a memory of childhood. Such that in the end we can only agree with Vasari: in the case of Piero, "science," far from jabbering mistakenly about art and being detrimental to it, was on the contrary well suited to develop its effects and expand its reach.

6

If the metaphor were admissible, and if a picture were indeed, as Alberti says, a window opening onto the outside world and through which one looks at what is painted there, the operation of painting still would not be reducible to a mere framing, any more than to a description, more or less elaborate, of all or some of the elements of the whole constituted thereby. We would still have reason to expect the preparatory act to mark it in a way that would demonstrate how the given of the window conflates, axiomatically, with the fact of its opening—or to put this differently, how the definition of the picture must constantly reference its initial delimitation. The "open" never being a settled matter in what carries out its operation, having to maintain itself as an opening that is, so to speak, continuous, permanent, like divine creation for Descartes and the revolution for Trotsky[1]; from the *Città Ideale* in Urbino (long attributed to Piero della Francesca or his circle) to *Las Meninas* by Velàsquez, the economy of classic representation never offering itself more fully to vision than in the moment of its suspension, and without one's even being able to decide whether the curtain has just risen on the still empty scene that it reveals, or if on the contrary it is about to fall again, the representation having come full term. Or, what amounts to the same thing, whether the painter of *Las Meninas*, his brush suspended in the air, is moving closer to his canvas or is on the contrary backing away from it.[2]

This same notion of opening holds, *mutatis mutandis,* for the scene of the dream, when the dreamer dreams that he awakens from it. As in the classic example, such as Freud recounts it, of the dream of the Wolf Man:

I dreamt that it was night and that I was lying in my bed. (My bed stood with its foot towards the window; in front of the window there was a row of old walnut trees. I know it was winter when I had the dream, and night-time.) Suddenly the window opened of its own accord, and I was terrified to see that some white wolves were sitting on the big walnut tree in front of the window. There were six or seven of them. The wolves were quite white, and looked more like foxes or sheep-dogs, for they had big tails like foxes and they had their ears pricked like dogs when they pay attention to something. In great terror, evidently of being eaten up by the wolves, I screamed and woke up.

And the patient adds almost immediately:

The only piece of action in the dream was the opening of the window; for the wolves sat quite still and without making any movement on the branches of the tree, to the right and left of the trunk, and looked at me.[3]

The eponymous figure in the *Madonna del Parto* does not look at the viewer, enclosed as she seems to be in her own dream and occupied only with the event of which her body is the site, at an insurmountable distance (an image, to quote Jean-Luc Godard again, of the contradiction that makes the subject interesting: Why can't we get close to the Virgin?[4]). But if there must be a viewer here, he would not necessarily be troubled by Mary's appellation "Mother of God" (*Maria die Gottesgebärerin*), as was Freud's famous patient at the time of his infantile neurosis[5] (as might have been, too, in a wholly different context and in wholly different terms, some of Piero's contemporaries?), nor made to experience by the same token, in her internal oven, the ambivalent feelings toward the father that Freud claimed were an underlying factor in all religions,[6] and—one is tempted to add—especially in monotheistic religions about whose monotheism, precisely, there is something unbearable, something that regularly elicits a kind of multiplication, Trinitarian or other: children, as Freud says straight out, often being seemingly even better than adults at detecting, with relentless logic, the weaknesses and contradictions of the sacred fiction.[7] And yet, however indifferent he or she might be to religious matters, and more or less ignorant of

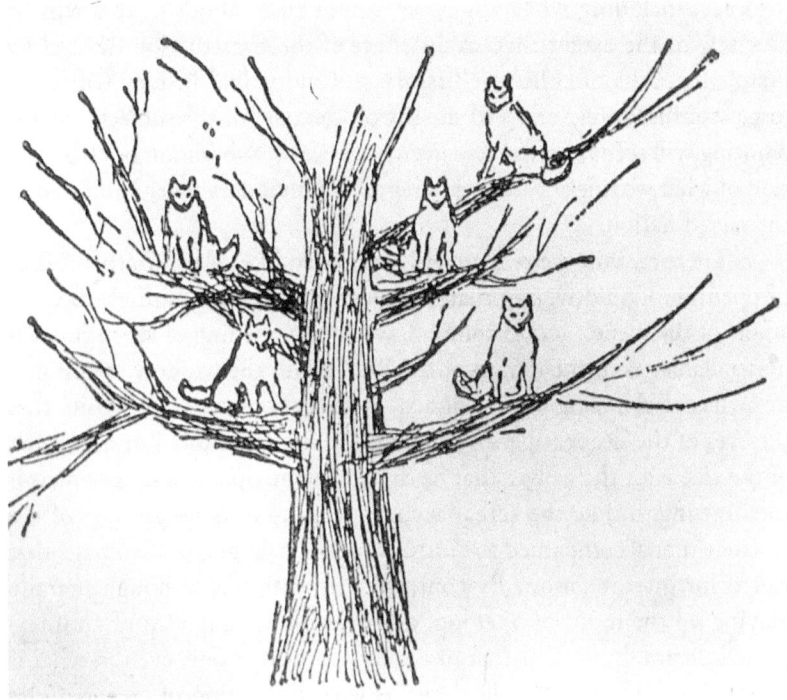

6.1. Dream of the Wolf Man, after Freud, *GW*, 12:55.

theological questions, the icon of the pregnant Virgin cannot help but awaken in any adult subject of European education who today enters into its spirit and surrenders to its enterprise, even more so than a feeling of its belonging to a world profoundly marked by the biblical tradition, a prescience of the obscure connection that this devotional image, which seems to sum up part of the Christian mystery, is capable of maintaining with the most archaic strata of his own psychic constitution.

The discrepancy that it would perhaps be advisable to note between the way that masculine subjects and feminine subjects broach the *Madonna del Parto* still does not justify conflating the male and female positions with the distinctive traits of masculinity and femininity such as these are found in the one and the other sex.[8] So much so that if the metaphor of the childhood memory has any pertinence in the present instance, including what might be "sublimated" about it, this will be precisely to the extent that, as an effect of the construction devised by Piero, the paths of collective history and individual history will seem to get confused, regardless of the sex or "gender" of the subject—as the painting will seem to effect a convergence of the elaboration or construction of what we might call, by analogy, "childhood memory" and that of the sacred fiction.

There remain the two angels, positioned like velarii, in their office of opening. Could we say that, however "suspended" it might be, the whole of the scene's action comes down to the opening of the tent, itself undecidable, as in the dream of the Wolf Man, the window opening of its own accord having been included, in the patient's view, to signify that the eyes of the sleeper opened suddenly—a datum ignored in the sketch of the tree with the wolves that he drew to shore up his description: as if the drawing, unlike the verbal account, could brook no glimpse of the violence that accompanied the intrusion, in the dream, of the image that called for interpretation? By contrast, Piero's fresco, although literally playing on the motif of opening, does not induce any idea of an unexpected dream, but rather that of a vision as such at one, even in what is most manifestly remarkable about it, with the notion of an indefinite suspension, halfway between veiling and unveiling. If there is any action on the part of the two angels, it is inseparable from their simultaneously supple and frozen symmetry. To say nothing of the other gesture, no less conspicuous, even ostentatious, that likewise attracts the attention of all who look, whether man or woman. But gesture is saying too much: if what seems to be on the order of a mere light touching happens to make a sign, this is not so much through its restraint, equivocal to say the least, as through its location, which is by no means ambiguous.

The question that many art historians ultimately put to themselves, concerning the *Madonna del Parto,* is not so much what it "represents" or "means" as what sort of status it has as object, insofar as the thing is definable. "Thing" or "object": here's what we're dealing with in this "Virgin-tabernacle," this image that turns the expectant Virgin into an object meant to be first of all (an ordering of priorities that itself raises questions) a cult object. But an image—likewise—that, whatever one might wish, is connected to the "thing" that most accounts which take it to be, precisely, an object make a point of repressing. As object and, simultaneously, as image of the mother, the *Madonna del Parto* effectively references (without there being any need whatever to postulate a connection between Piero's work and his maternal ancestry) what for both sexes alike is the prototype of all object relations, the function defined by Winnicott as that of the mother's seeming to be decisive in the child's primary apprehension of reality. And this, I must insist, in a situation characterized as pre-Oedipal, and thus applicable to girls as well as boys: the phallic stage, so-called because before sexual differentiation there is only one representation of the genital state, namely the phallus as such, its erect image—the object around which turns the whole dialectic of individual development, the major misunderstandings of infantile sexual theories coming down, in Freud's view, to the child's having no notion either of the vagina, or of sperm, or of generation in general.[9] The essential thing still being that all imaginary relations (and it is indeed a partly imaginary relation that the viewer maintains with images, beginning with the one of the phallic mother that he imagines his expectant mother to be) are modeled after the fundamental relation between mother and child, however problematic, including the positions one might be tempted to assign to its principals, whereas everything suggests that what's in question is a real relation.[10]

Seeing as what's in question is the imaginary relation that can arise between an image of the mother in painting and an adult subject, himself caught in, or better yet *drawn into,* something that claims to be a "history," whether his own or the one recounted by the gospels, be they apocryphal or of the moment of collective history in whose context the encounter with the image occurs, what about—all sex or gender differences being set aside, as is warranted by the "childhood memory" motif—the imaginary capture to which can give rise an image of a woman as mother-to-be, as future mother (and thus future Eve), and that designates—how to say this? that indicates, signals, shows, evokes (the hesitation over terms is telling)—at the same time that it covers it, the key site through which this to-come must pass: that is, the site where the baby is supposed to be found, below the double envelope of a robe and an undergarment (to say nothing of the tent), and from which it will emerge, as is explicitly indicated by the standard title of the image, but without this emergence providing any answer, save in the terms of faith, to the question as to *where it came from,* and who its father is? But a site, too, around which turns the question of the presence/absence of the imaginary object which is the phallus, Lacan's demonstration obviously holding for the *Madonna del Parto,* considered precisely as object, in the triple sense already mentioned: art object and/or cult object such as it's the business of historians and theologians to know; but symbolic object, first of all, through the detour of the maternal *imago,* which is related precisely, even in its most "sublimated" recurrences (the *Madonna del Parto* being a preeminent example), to the most obscure and primary ground of object relations. If there is an "opening" Virgin in this instance, what does it open onto? Not an image of the Trinity, as essentially masculine image[11]; and not the maternal breast, the primary love object, as for example in the Santo Spirito altarpiece by Botticelli (whose relation to Piero's Virgin seems indisputable), but the site of an (imaginary) absence as much as of a presence that for its part is symbolic. Woman does not have a phallus; but not to have it, symbolically, is to participate in it as absence, and thus in some sense to have it—which defines, as Lacan also says, the beyond of all object relations.

The *Madonna del Parto* offers nothing to vision except herself: she gives her*self* to vision, the way she presents herself to the viewer corresponding to the reflexive, middle tense of the verb. But that's because in terms of having—and of being visible? [*d'avoir / d'à-voir*]—she has nothing but the baby, which is for her a substitute for the phallus, its symbolic equivalent, but which she cannot exhibit as such, which she can only *signify* by this gesture that is not even one of designation or monstration, this gesture that hides as much as it shows, this gesture that shows while hiding, this hand that plays on the opposition between presence and absence, having and not having, as well as between modesty and immodesty. Giovanni Pozzi saw well, in this regard, that the garment with inverted pleats given to the Virgin is one of the most original features of the *Madonna del Parto,* like the hand that simultaneously covers and indicates.[12] For what's in question is not so much hiding the object as hiding its lack: garments serve to hide not only what one *has* but also what one *doesn't have.* The paradox, with the *Madonna del Parto,* being that her robe seems to open in order to *show*. But to show what, if not the very fact of the opening insofar as this intensifies the question of the object, which is also the question of the baby insofar as this might be taken to equal the phallus in the subject's unconscious, especially that of women?

Which is to say that the garment takes part in the same relation of interposition as a veil or a curtain hung in front of something, which must be acknowledged as one of the fundamental images (I say advisedly: one of the *images*) of the relation to the world. In the words of Lacan:

> With the presence of a curtain, what is beyond as lack tends to realize itself as image. On the veil is painted absence. This is just the function of any curtain whatever. The curtain derives its value, its being, and its consistency precisely from being that onto which absence is projected and imagined. The curtain is, so to speak, the idol of absence.[13]

And how not to think here, yet again, of Alberti's "veil," of the *velum* that the author of *Della pittura* advised painters to interpose between their eyes and the object that they were to paint: a transparent fabric that functions like an equivalent of the plane intersecting the visual pyramid supposedly corresponding to the picture, and onto which one need only transfer by transparency the object's outlines to obtain, almost mechanically, a simulacrum consistent with the rules of linear perspective; but not without there being indicated, by the same token, a beyond of the object (of the figure) related, precisely, to the perspective construction conceived as model or paradigm of representation?

It is not only the tent, with its two flaps lifted like those of a curtain, which, despite the involuted construction of the scene and the attendant foreclosure of an outside, that is consistent with what Lacan calls the relation of *interposition,* which means that what is loved in the object is always something situated beyond the said object: a "nothing," but one that nonetheless has the property of being there, symbolically, and that can and must be this nothing because it is a symbol—which is the very definition of the fetish.[14] Doubtless the *Madonna del Parto* does not have the "mysteriously iconic and even idolatrous" quality that Longhi discerned in Piero's early *Madonna della Misericordia,* the central panel of a polyptych commissioned from the painter in 1445 by fellow citizens belonging to the eponymous religious confraternity.[15] Although there is a clear analogy between the Virgin-tabernacle of Monterchi and the Virgin who shelters the devout under her ample azure mantle with mauve lining, reference to an outside imposes itself in this conventional and eminently protective figure of piety, inscribed against a uniform gold ground. Whereas the quilted fabric that constitutes, in Monterchi, the lining of the tent is indeed the "idol of absence" mentioned by Lacan.

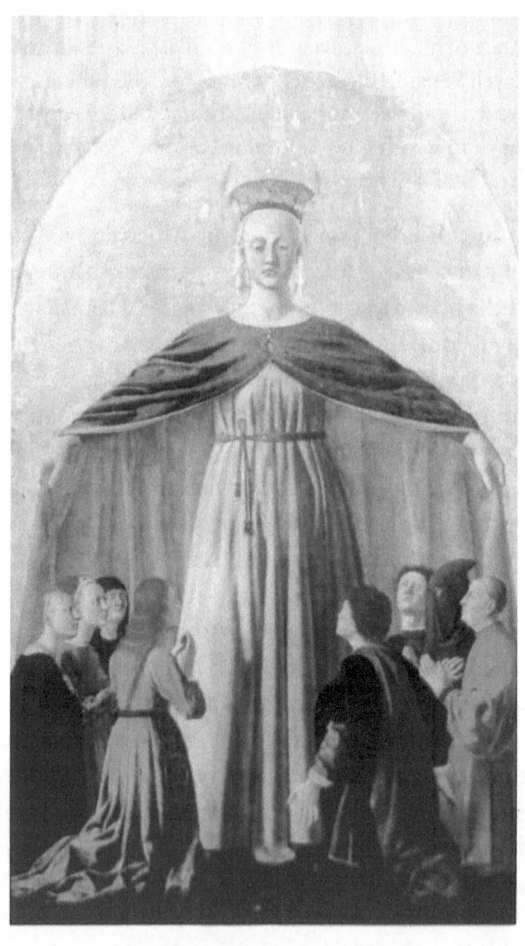

6.2. Piero della Francesca, *Madonna della Misericordia Polyptych*, central panel, Borgo San Sepolcro.

If there is a veil here, it does not interpose itself between the viewer and the figure that it envelops. Freud, Lacan further notes, assimilated the fetish to a memorial or monument (*Denkmal*) that had been set up (*aufrecht zu halten*), as we would say of a decor.[16] In the same way that Piero set up, against a background that everything suggests was strictly decorative, the monument that is the fresco of Monterchi: beginning with the tent, decorated as it is with brocade pomegranates (at once a nuptial and a fertility symbol[17]) and lined with fur (at least according to a description adhering to the one of the tent of the tabernacle in the Old Testament). Whereby the painter only succeeded in playing, in paradoxical fashion, on the appearance of a perspective construction to the end of signifying not so much the object's outside as its beyond, the vanishing point—or its imaginary substitute, which would have to be called its *fiction*—apparently having been dispatched outside the field, along the vertical, as an effect of the calculated convergence (which has nothing to do [*rien à voir*] with the receding lines perpendicular to the picture plane) of the quilting lines. This would lead one to connect this image of the Virgin of childbirth not so much to a Visitation as to an Annunciation understood as the moment of the descent, into the Virgin's womb, of the divine seed. A descent, if there is such, that is symbolic, even in its obligatory up-setting of the perspective configuration from horizontal to vertical, the vanishing point (or its fiction) being in this case radically discrepant from the "point of view" with which it becomes conflated when, under allegedly normal conditions, the perspective operation is tied down to an earthly horizon[18]—which horizon is missing from the *Madonna del Parto*, the scene's construction precluding any outside at the same time that it seems to be focused on the high place of the divine by the dissimulation of a vertical projection *da sù in sotto,* downward.[19]

The "awkwardness" that Focillon thought he discerned in the composition of the *Madonna del Parto*[20] doubtless had something to do with the paradox of this construction, which is rigorously involuted but which nonetheless signals, on the bias of an illusionist transcendence, toward a beyond where the key to the mystery would be found (but a key that is useless as regards the archaic, fantasy-based questioning with which the work reconnects, and from which it derives a portion of its power), the relation to a beyond being fundamental to the establishment of any symbolic relation.[21] To which I would add that the reference to a transcendental beyond, albeit acquired by strictly illusionist means, has the effect here of relativizing the involution of the image: if immortality as well as perfection consist, as Plato already maintained,[22] in having no relation to an outside, this still doesn't hold for the Virgin as much as it does for God. But what would God be if he had to let himself be

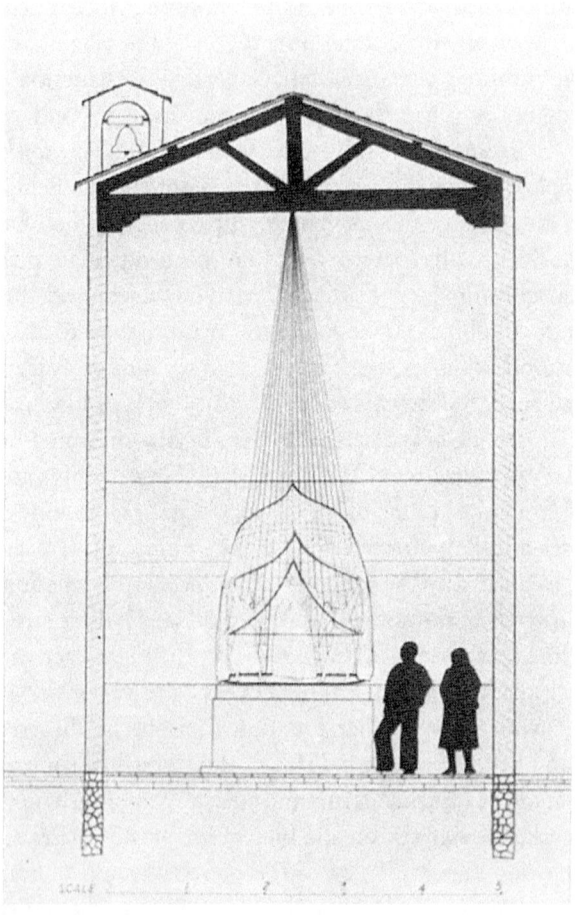

6.3. *Madonna del Parto*: perspective fiction of the beyond, after Martone in *Convegno*, p. 94.

assigned an image, in the sense this term is used in projective geometry: a point, albeit one sent, as in Piero's configuration, *quasi per infinito?* But the real paradox lies elsewhere. It resides in the fact that whereas we might well expect a book placed, like the one you've just read, under the sign of a "childhood memory" to end with a construction in good and proper form, one that would restore—in Freud's own words—"an image trustworthy and in all essential respects complete" (*ein zuverlässiges und in allen wesentlichen Stücken vollständig Bild*)[23] of the forgotten past of which this "fantasy" (as Freud calls it) is a kind of index or substitute (an *Ersatz*), in the end the reader comes to know, at the term assigned the analysis by the constraints which are those of writing and publication, only the construction adhered to by the image that is the work's essential concern. To an extent that might seem to turn upside down the comparison introduced by Freud between the work of construction, which is the task of the analyst, and that of the archeologist who strives to restore, starting from the fragments he has managed to uncover, the appearance of a building long since destroyed and buried, going so far as to reconstitute the decorations that once adorned the walls on the basis of the recovered debris.[24] Freud taking care to note that things go differently for monuments from the past and for the psychic object whose prehistory the analyst wants to gather up, that although the archeologist deals with objects whose integral wholes are irretrievably lost, that's not the way it works with psychic formations: "Here we are regularly met by a situation which with the archeological object occurs only in such rare circumstances as those of Pompeii or of the tomb of Tut'ankhamun. All of the essentials are preserved; even things that seem completely forgotten are present somehow and somewhere, and have merely been buried and made inaccessible to the subject."[25]

Faced with the *Madonna del Parto,* the historian (or whatever one wants to call him) finds himself in a singular position. Only a part of Piero's fresco has come down to us, and the scant available remains scarcely allow us to form an idea of the ground on which it was inscribed, the figure of the Virgin under its dais probably having been preserved solely for reasons of economy.[26] But the task incumbent upon him is nonetheless like that of the analyst in that, far from having to model himself after the rhythm of the *giornate* imposed by the medium of fresco, and thus necessarily having to complete one phase of the work before passing to the next one—as, according to Freud, in the construction of a house, where the walls must be put up and the windows placed before beginning to decorate the interior of the rooms—both kinds of work proceed in tandem, the one being always a step ahead, the other following soon after.[27] The comparison should be taken literally here, including the role assigned the placing of the "windows" and the installation of the decor: if, in the matter of art, the two enterprises are to be pursued together, this is not only because analysis should remain as close as possible to the construction that it is its responsibility to reveal; it is also, and perhaps preeminently, because the construction cannot be separated from the decor and is an integral part of it, being by intent decorative, while the decor should itself be "set up."

In fact, everything happens as though, through an up-setting analogous to the one imposed on the perspective configuration, the intention of the fiction here were, if not to assume the function which is that of the analyst, then at least to occupy his place, the viewer (even if a believer) being called upon to undergo the trial of a work that will find its justification only when the construction, somewhere, has hit its mark, the effect being commensurate with the artifice from which it springs. Somewhere, which is to say where necessary: in the unconscious, each individual playing his part on the scene or stage that is his own, as happens in the work of analysis.[28] What we should retain from Freud, in this instance, is the seemingly paradoxical idea of a *double scene or stage* that would be, as here, the mainspring of the analysis. That the scene established by the work of art and on which it operates should be related to the place assigned the viewer, this is what the configuration of classic representation wants, playing as it does not only on the division of roles but also on the marked difference between the scene or stage and the viewing space [*scène . . . salle*]. But the fact that, in Freud's description of the work of analysis, the position allotted to the analyst is just as readily assimilable to a *scene or stage* as is the one assigned to the patient is sufficient indication that here we are dealing with something very different from a representation. Quite apart from the fact that it is not the analyst's function to remember anything, his task being, the rules of the game having been established, to ensure that the subject accepts having his own text, his own scenario, his own "play" come from the Other. The connection between the two portions, plays, or pieces (*Stücke*) of the work of analysis, the work of remembering and that of interpretation, being secured by the constructions that the analyst communicates to the analysand at what he deems the right moment, and by the explanations with which he accompanies them.[29] Freud preferred the term *construction* to that of interpretation. The reason being, he said (finding the distinction sufficient to indicate the distance between the intent of analysis and that of hermeneutics), that interpretation never concerns itself with anything but isolated elements or traits, whereas construction faces up to the function of making connections: connections between the bits and pieces of material that are the concern of analysis; but connections, too, between the two pieces or plays (the two monologues) that are played out on the two mutually present scenes or stages. The said construction attaining its goal when, from one stage or scene or monologue to the other, communication is established, and something like "truth" manages to come to light. Which is tantamount to saying, to return to the esthetic relation, that the unconscious to which the work appeals, through its very construction, will come into play, will enter the picture, only through the mediation of the viewer or interpreter. In the normal conditions of reception, the effect will be produced only belatedly [*après coup*], the essential part of the work of interpretation being accomplished in the work's absence. It's up to the interpreter to play his part, and to see to his own unconscious, making a special effort to remember what might have been forgotten, even repressed, during the encounter with the work, however intense and prolonged, even repeated, it might have been.

If the configuration devised by Piero della Francesca, if the constructive artifice that is the mainspring of the *Madonna del Parto* presents many analogies with a childhood memory, this is first of all because the primary material that it mobilizes is, by its nature, akin to the substance of the "fantasies about their childhood that people construct at a late date" ("*die spät geschaffenen Phantasien der Menschen über ihre Kindheit lennen*").[30] Now this raw material, this *Rohstoff* can indeed manifest itself, depending on place, period, and individual, in various forms;

nonetheless, it obeys laws of formation that are, at the deepest level, the common lot of humanity. Except, again, that if the idea of creation or even fabrication is clearly affirmed, dealing as we are with a memory of childhood, we still cannot speak of a *construction* that, as such, is deliberate: the generative connotation of the term *schaffen* instead being sufficient to underscore its enigmatic character.

The fable that Vasari invented or collected about Piero's childhood and the literally premature death of his father indicates a problem. A problem, as was said at the outset, related to the one with which Freud began in his analysis of the Leonardo "case," although in the opposite direction: How did artistic creation and scientific investigation manage to coexist so happily in this painter, whereas after the early Renaissance, by contrast, artistic culture and esthetic theory, Vasari first and foremost, strove to make them seem like enemies? To the extent that one might be tempted to see in the fable itself, at the cost of an anachronism that historians would rush to denounce, a kind of "construction" that aimed to account for Piero's destiny in quasi-analytic terms. As it happens, neither the few documents available to us pertaining to the painter nor his own writings offer any elements that would make it possible, through a construction such as Freud undertook with regard to Leonardo da Vinci, to give some thickness to his "artist's life," and analysis cannot pretend in this instance to "take hold of biography," in accordance with the wish that was Freud's. All that it can aim to do (and this is not nothing) is to respond, in the terms that are its own, to what, in the work, summons up even now in the viewer, whether man or woman, believer or miscreant, the sudden emergence of the subject as such. The effect, yet again, being commensurate with the artifice from which it springs.

Whether it is a question of the "term" imposed on the perspective construction or of the projective fiction under cover of which reference is introduced to a beyond of the object posited as divine, the work of "science" and that of art would, in order to come together, have had to follow the paths that are those of sublimation. Now the same goes for the inflection here introduced to the maternal *imago*. To pretend to treat the *Madonna del Parto* as a memory of childhood—or to put it better, as an image that would work with givens and in forms analogous to those of a memory of childhood—is not just a matter of finding there, in highly sublimated guise, the echo of a memory in some sense "generic": the human species recognizing itself, let us repeat after Freud, in the mystery that for it represents generation as well as the sexual difference that is its condition. The echo effect springing not only from the Virgin's rounded belly, any more than from the hand that simultaneously covers and designates the open vent in the robe, but from the construction as a whole, which as such eludes interpretation: the genius of Piero consisting, as has been said, in giving ideogrammatic force to the enigma in which the Christian mystery participates without for all that merging with it, and which it in fact sums up but incompletely. Doing this, the painter not only summons up, through the detour of this construction without an outside, the advent of the subject as subject of its own individual history. In the indefinite suspension from which it springs, this image of waiting pertains, in figurative terms, to the same operation as the one to which Freud compared the production of a childhood memory: that of written history when, not content with sticking to a chronicle of events in the present tense, it pretends to reconnect with a nation's mythic or legendary origins. The history of earliest days responding in his view to the same need as the sexual theories of children: that of learning where we come from and how we come to be.[31]

The fact that the question is here posed in the terms—if not in the forms—which are those of Christian iconography changes nothing. However original, even incongruous, it might be, the image of this Virgin of childbirth is directly related to the event inscribed at the outset of Christian history at the same time that, in the visible guise of the tabernacle, it figures the New Covenant: Holy Writ—whatever its ultimate core of historical truth, as with legends of origin, if not madness itself[32]—being traversed from end to end by the question of the Father, and of his name. The fact that, in this foundational image, the Virgin is shown on the point of giving birth references a mystery henceforth specified as Christian (monstration, as both Heidegger and Wittgenstein would have it, belonging to what is most originary in "saying," if not in "writing"): that of the Incarnation, intensified as it is by that of the intact virginity of this mother-to-be, which virginity cannot for its part be the object of any monstration, any more than of any figuration, but must remain an article of faith.[33] The image nonetheless derives its power from the fact that it plays simultaneously on the elaboration, by Christian culture, of the history of its own origins and on the recollection, by individuals, of their most archaic past. And more than this: on the fact that the scene it establishes functions as a place of exchange, a *shared space* [*lieu commun*] at the junction or hinge of Sacred History and individual experience.

"Recollection of the history [*histoire*] stops at the moment just before"[34]: so much so that if there is indeed a stop in this instance, it cannot, strictly speaking, be regarded as a freeze frame—save by putting the image back into a continuous chain or sequence, as Freud tried to do with the *Moses* by Michelangelo. The stop is a stop of history, or of its recollection, despite the fact that the waiting accrues the whole of its meaning only by referencing the announcement in which it participates even in its suspension, in this case not of an instant but of a posing time whose length is undetermined. In this regard, the *Madonna del Parto* goes the way of the unconscious. Rather than outside of history, it stands "outside of time."[35] Outside of the time which is that of history, but also outside of the biological time which would be that of gestation. Caught in the moment of the *before,* of which there can be no representation—from the moment that the event to which it refers is decidedly against nature—save one that is caught in the spatiality proper to the Signifier, whether by way of writ (holy or otherwise) or of its substitutes and variants, its iconic manifestations.

What, in effect, could be more contrary to the notion of nature than the operation of the Holy Spirit, and this as much with regard to the exigencies that might be those of adult thought as to the questions of a child—the Holy Spirit that, as Lacan professes, is "the entry of the signifier into the world"?[36] Piero della Francesca said of perspective that "its very name says how to designate things seen from afar, represented against certain given 'terms' in proportion, according to their distance."[37] It remains to find a name for a mode of analysis that would aim not so much to translate into discursive terms the message or "signified" which is that of a work like the *Madonna del Parto* as to consider it for what it is, including the distance at which it operates, as both vestige from a vanished past and full-fledged "stage" or "scene": an image of the entry of the signifier into painting—or its entry *onto the scene* [*en scène*].

Elsewhere I have used the tag "analytic iconology" to introduce a discourse pertaining to works of art that, rejecting any notion of "applied psychoanalysis" but making its own the hypothesis of the unconscious, would have at its center the question of figurability, of *Darstellbarkeit* in Freud's sense: that is, the condition to which is subjugated all thought that seeks to come to light in art as in dreams, but that can manage this only by acceding in one way or another to visibility.[38] At the risk, precisely, of seeing the unconscious arise where we didn't expect it.[39] It is not easy, in the matter of art, to distinguish between what Freud, citing Leonardo da Vinci, called "the reasons [*ragioni*] of Nature"[40] and the reasons that might be those of the signifier, any more than it is between the reasons that might be those of culture or thought and those of the unconscious. To speak one last time as he himself does at the end of his Leonardo essay, every one of us human beings, of whatever stripe, who tries to see a bit more clearly how works of art operate embodies one of the countless perspectives that are detours whereby the one and the other of these reasons clears a path through experience.

Notes

ABBREVIATIONS OF FREQUENTLY CITED SOURCES

Battisti   Eugenio Battisti, *Piero della Francesca,* Milan, 1971.

Bertelli   Carlo Bertelli, *Piero della Francesca* (1991), trans. Edward
                Farelly, New Haven, Yale University Press, 1992.

Convegno   *Convegno internazionale sulla "Madonna del Parto" di Piero
                della Francesca,* Monterchi, 1980.

Freud/Leonardo Sigmund Freud, "Eine Kinderheitserinnerung des Leonardo
                da Vinci" (1910), *GW,* vol. 7, pp. 127–211; English translation
                "Leonardo da Vinci and a Memory of His Childhood," *SE,*
                vol. 11, pp. 63–137.

Giorni   Bruno Giorni, *La Madonna del Parto di Piero della Franc-
                esca,* San Sepolcro, 1977. Second, expanded edition 1989.

GW   Sigmund Freud, *Gesammelte Werke,* 17 volumes, London,
                Imago Press, 1940–1952.

Longhi   Roberto Longhi, *Piero della Francesca* (1927), trans. David
                Tabbat, Riverdale-on-Hudson: Stanley Moss/Sheep
                Meadow Books, 2002. Volume 3 of the complete works of
                Longhi, published in Florence in 1980, gathers all of his
                writings on Piero, as does the English translation of this
                volume, which I cite in my notes.

Pozzi   Giovanni Pozzi, "Maria Tabernacolo," in *Italia medioevale
                e umanistica,* vol. 32 (1989), pp. 263–326.

Restauro   *Piero della Francesca. La Madonna del Parto. Restauro e
                iconografia.* Venice, 1993.

SE   Sigmund Freud, *The Standard Edition of the Complete
                Psychological Works of Sigmund Freud, translated from the
                German under the General Editorship of James Strachey
                in collaboration with Anna Freud,* 24 volumes. London:
                Hogarth Press and Institute of Psycho-Analysis, 1953–1973.

CHAPTER I

1. Meyer Schapiro, "Leonardo and Freud: An Art-Historical Study" (1956), in idem, *Theory and Philosophy of Art: Style, Artist, and Society* (New York: Braziller, 1994), pp. 153–92.

2. Freud/Leonardo, *GW,* 141ff; *SE,* 74ff. [Translation altered: *SE* renders *Wissensdrang* as "thirst for knowledge."]

3. The idea that "incompletion" (not to be confused with the *non finito*) might be the most salient feature of the "exemplary" case that Leonardo represented for Freud, insofar as it was thought to arise from an inhibition at the execution stage, dates from the most imperious moment of psychoanalysis. The one when its creator could write to Jung: "I am glad you share my belief that we must conquer the whole field of mythology." Adding that, apart from the vistas opened up by Rank and Abraham, they needed workers for more far-reaching campaigns. Such was also the case, according to him, for another domain: "We must also take hold of biography." In this connection, Freud did not hesitate to report, in this same letter, on his analysis of the Leonardo "case," which he regarded as a first step in this direction: "I have had an inspiration since my return. The riddle of Leonardo da Vinci's character has suddenly become clear to me . . . But the material concerning L[eonardo] is so sparse that I despair of demonstrating my conviction intelligibly to others." But if he was then waiting impatiently for a book that would provide him with more information about Leonardo's youth, this was not to verify the validity of his interpretation and to obtain additional support for it, but only to make it more convincing. For the "secret" thought that he then saw fit to reveal to Jung was this: "Do you remember my remarks in the 'Sexual Theories of Children' (2nd *Short Papers*) to the effect that children's first primitive researches in this sphere were bound to fail and that this first failure could have a paralyzing effect on them? Read the passage over; at the time I did not take it as seriously as I do now. Well, the great Leonardo was such a man; at an early age he converted his sexuality into a craving for knowledge and from then on a pattern of not finishing anything [*die Vorbildlichkeit des nicht Fertigwerdens*] to which he had to conform in all his ventures: he was sexually inactive or homosexual." Letter to C.-G. Jung, October 17, 1909, in S. Freud and C.-G. Jung, *The Freud/Jung Letters: The Correspondence Between Sigmund Freud and C. G. Jung,* ed. William McGuire, trans. Ralph Manheim and R.F.C. Hull (Princeton: Princeton University Press, 1974), p. 255 [translation altered]. Which amounts to recognizing here a symptom, a pathological trait, and perhaps more than that: the index of a "method" in Valéry's sense of the word?

4. Longhi, 180.

5. When (I can't wait) will we see a reconstruction of Piero's *Flagellation* in a wax museum?

6. Longhi, 15.

7. Thomas Martone, "Piero della Francesca e la prospettiva dell'intelletto," in *Piero teorico dell'arte*, ed. Omar Calabrese (Rome, 1985), figs. 60–64.

8. Millard Meiss, "La Sacra Conversazione di Piero della Francesca," *Quaderni di Brera 1* (Florence, 1971). On the question of the egg and for remarks supplementary to the 1971 article, cf. M. Meiss, *The Painter's Choice: Problems in the Interpretation of Renaissance Art* (New York: Harper & Row, 1976), pp. 105–47.

9. "*Egli per reverenza, rizzatosi a sedere sul letto, contando il mal suo e gli accidenti di quello, mostrava tuttavia quanto aveva offeso Dio e gli uomini del mondo, non avendo operato nell'arte come si conveniva.*" G. Vasari, "Vita di Leonardo da Vinci," in *Le Vite de' piu eccellenti pittori, scultori e architettori*, 2nd ed. (Florence, 1568); Milanesi ed. (Milan, 1879), vol. 4, p. 49 ["Wherefore he, out of reverence, having raised himself to sit upon the bed, giving him an account of his sickness and the circumstances of it, showed withal how much he had offended God and mankind in not having worked at his art as he should have done." *Lives* 1:639]; cited by Freud/Leonardo, *GW*, 129; *SE*, 64.

10. Freud/Leonardo, *GW*, 129; *SE*, 63.

11. "They [the princes of Urbino] themselves produce in painting the first duke of Urbino, a young man who was killed by his subjects for his injustice; he was not of this lineage," *Journal de voyage de Montaigne*, ed. F. Rigolot (Paris, 1992), p. 148. This note proves, contra Carlo Ginzberg, that the traditional interpretation according to which the *Flagellation* was related to the assassination, on orders from Federico de Montefeltre, of his young brother Odantonio during the conspiracy of 1444 originated long before the eighteenth century (cf. Ginzburg, *The Enigma of Piero: Piero della Francesca: The Baptism, the Arezzo Cycle, the Flagellation* (1981), trans. Martin Ryle and Kate Soper (London: Verso, 1985), pp. 116–17.

12. Cf. Jean-Pierre Vernant, "The Tragic Subject: Historicity and Transhistoricity" (1979), in J.-P. Vernant and Pierre Vidal-Naquet, *Myth and Tragedy in Ancient Greece* (1986), trans. Janet Lloyd (New York: Zone Books, 1990), pp. 237–47.

13. R. Longhi, "Piero dei Franceschi e lo sviluppo della pintura veneziana," *L'Arte*, 1914, pp. 198–221, 241–56. Cf. also Longhi, 207, 244–45.

14. "*Sebbene colui che doveva con tutte le forze ignarsi di accrescergli gloria e nome, per aver appreso da lui tutto che sapeva, come empio e maligno cerco d'anullare il nome di Piero suo precettore, e usurpar quell'onore, che a colui solo si doveva per se stesso, publicando sotto suo nome proprio, cioè di fra Luca dal Borgo, tutte le fattiche di quel buon vecchio, il quale, oltre le scienze dette di sopra, fu eccellente nella*

pittura." *Vite,* 2:488 ["The very man who should have striven with all his might to increase the glory and fame of Piero, from whom he had learnt all that he knew, was impious and malignant enough to blot out the name of his teacher, and to usurp for himself the honour that was due to the other, publishing under his own name, Fra Luca dal Borgo, all the labours of that good old man, who, besides the sciences named above, was excellent in painting." *Lives,* 1:397]. On the importance in Vasari's *Lives* of the *name* and its acquisition, its defense, its illustration, cf. Paul Barolsky, *Why Mona Lisa Smiles and Other Tales by Vasari* (University Park [Penn.]: Pennsylvania State University Press, 1991), pp. 39ff.

15. Longhi, 208.

16. *"Ma de'tempi nostri intra quelli che hanno lasciata qualche memoria di quest'Arte, il primo di tempo, & che con miglior metodo e forma ne habbia scritto, è statto maestro Piero della Francesca dal Borgo a san Sepolcro, del quale habbiamo hoggi tre libri scritti a mano, eccellentissimi disegnati: & chi vuol conoscere l'eccellenza loro, vegga che Daniel Barbaro ne ha trascritto una gran parte nel suo libro della prospettiva . . . habbiamo in oltre queste regole ordinarie in compendio da Leonbattista Alberti, da Lionardo da Vinci, da Alberto Duro, Giovacchino Fortio, & Giovan Lencker, & Veceslao Gianizzero Norinbergense, il quale ha messi in Prospettiva li corpi regolari, & altri composti, si come fece Piero dal Borgo, se bene F. Luca gli stampo sotto suo nome."* Ignazio Danti, preface to *Le Due Regole della prospettiva practica* by Jacomo Barozzi (Rome, 1583).

17. Luigi Lanzi, *Storia pittorica della Italia: Dal risorgimento delle belle arti fin presso al fine del XVIII secolo* (Bassano, 1789); cited in Longhi, 219.

18. Alfred Woltmann and Karl Woermann, *Geschichte der malerei* (Leipzig, 1882), vol. 2, pp. 215–20; Bernard Berenson, *The Central Italian Painters* (London: P. Putnam's Sons, 1897), p. 69; Adolfo Venturi, *Storia dell'arte,* 11 vols. (Milan: U. Hoepli, 1911), vol. 7, part 1, p. 440.

19. Cf., e.g., Martin Kemp, "Leonardo and the Visual Pyramid," *Journal of the Warburg and Courtauld Institutes,* vol. 40 (1977), pp. 128–49; James Ackerman, "Leonardo's Eye," ibid., vol. 41 (1978), pp. 108–46, etc.

20. Cf. the preface to my *The Origin of Perspective* (1987), trans. John Goodman (Cambridge, Mass.: MIT Press, 1994), pp. xix–xxiv.

21. Longhi, 247. Cf. Leonardo Olschki, *Geschichte der neusprachlichen wissenschaftlichen Literatur,* 3 vols. (Heidelberg: C. Winter, 1918–1927), vol. 1, pp. 137–51.

22. Julius von Schlosser, *Künstlerprobleme der Frührenaissance. II. Piero della Francesca III. Paolo Uccello IV. Michelozzo und Alberti* (Vienna/Leipzig, 1933).

23. Benedetto Croce, *Guide to Esthetics* (1913), trans. Patrick Romanell (Indianapolis/Cambridge: Hackett, 1995), p. 15 [translation altered].

24. Ibid., p. 18 [translation altered].

25. Ibid., p. 10.

26. J. von Schlosser, op. cit. (see note 22), p. 13.

27. Ibid., p. 22.

28. Ibid., p. 13.

29. Cf. Thierry de Duve, *Au nom de l'art. Pour une archéologie de la modernité* (Paris: Éditions de minuit, 1989). Marcel Duchamp himself noted the chronological proximity of Freud's essay on Leonardo (1910) and the "readymade" *L.H.O.O.Q.* (1919), in which the *Mona Lisa* is outfitted with a mustache and a Van Dyke beard (cf. Reinhold Dohl, "Le non-sens de l'art contre la folie du temps," in *Mélusine. Cahiers du Centre de recherche sur le surréalisme,* no. 9, "Arp poète plasticien" (Lausanne: L'Âge d'homme, 1987), p. 209.

30. Schlosser, op. cit. (see note 22), pp. 1–2.

31. Ibid., p. 33.

32. Even so, Longhi was far from ascribing equal weight to the two aspects of Piero's interests, noting that "we ought not to believe Vasari when he tells us that Piero applied himself at a precocious age to the study of mathematics, if only because it is difficult to discover anyone, at least in his native San Sepolcro, who could have taken him beyond a rudimentary use of the abacus. Furthermore, since Piero was a painter by inclination, it would seem likely that he arrived at mathematics—in which he saw hidden the key to perspective—through the study of painting, and not the other way around" (Longhi, 174).

33. Cf. above, note 14.

34. *"Il quale essendo stato tenuto maestro raro nelle difficultà de'corpi regolari, et nell' aritmetica e geometria, non potette, sporaggiunto nella vecchiezza dalla cecità corporale e dalla fine della vita, mandare in luce le virtuose fatiche sue."* Vasari, "Vita di Piero della Francesca," *Vite,* 487 ["He, having been held a rare master of the difficulties of drawing regular bodies, as well as of arithmetic and geometry, was yet not able—being overtaken in his old age by the infirmity of blindness—to bring to light his noble labors." *Lives,* 1:397].

35. Berto degli Alberti, "Codicetto di memorie, con citazione relativa a Piero," extract published by G. degli Azzi in *Archivi della Storia d'Italia* IV (Rocca san Casciano, 1915), as cited in Longhi, 188.

36. Parma, Palatine Library, cod. 1576 (in Italian). The Latin version is in the Biblioteca Ambrosiana, Milan. Cod. 5 P 6 *bis.*

37. Gerolamo Mancini, "L'opera 'De corporibus regularibus' di Pietro Franceschi detto della Francesca," *Atti della Reale Academia dei Lincei—Memorie della classe di Scienze Morali Storiche e Filologiche,* ser. 5, vol. 14 (Rome, 1915), pp. 446–87; cited in Longhi, 187–88 and 246.

38. See the arguments advanced along these lines in Bertelli, 38.

39. *"Attese Pietro nella sua giovanezza alle mathematiche, ed ancora che di anni quindici fusse in diritto a essere pittore, non si ritrasse pero mai da quelle: anzi, facendo maravigliosi frutto ed in quelle e nella pittura, fu adoperato da Guidobaldo Feltre, duc vecchio d'Urbino . . . Vi si conservano alcuni suoi scritti de cose di geometria e di prospettive, nelle quali non fu inferiore a niuno de'tempi suoi ne forse che sia stato in altri tempi giammai; come ne dimostrano tutte l'opere sue piene di prospettive, e particolare un vaso in modo tirato a quadri e facce, che si vede dinanzi, di dietro, et dagli lati il fondo e la bocca: il che è certo cosa stupenda, avendo in quello sottilmente tirato ogni minutia, e fatto scortare il girare di tutti que'circoli con molta grazia."* Vasari, "Vita di Pietro della Francesca," *Vite,* 490–91 [*Lives,* 1:397–98].

40. *"Fu Piero, come si è detto, studiossimo dell'arte, e si esercito assai nella prospettiva, ed ebbe buonissima cognizione d'Euclide, in tanto che tutti i migliori giri tirati ne'corpi regolari, egli meglio che altro geometra intense, ed i maggior lumi che di tal cosa ci siano, son di sua mano."* *Vite,* 498 [*Lives,* 1:401].

41. Longhi, 11.

42. "He left a daughter . . . and a wife, who was wont to say that Paolo would stay in his study [*nello scrittoio*] all night, seeking to solve the problems of perspective [*per trovar i termini della prospettiva*], and that when she called him to come to bed, he would say: 'Oh, what a sweet thing is this perspective!' [*Oh che dolce cosa è questa prospettiva!*] And in truth, if it was sweet to him, it was not otherwise than dear and useful, thanks to him, to those who exercised themselves therein after his time." *Vite,* 2:217 [*Lives,* 1:289].

43. Christiane Klapisch-Zuber, *La Maison et le Nom. Stratégies et rituels dans l'Italie de la Renaissance* (Paris, 1983), pp. 28–29.

44. Cf. Margaret Daly Davis, *Piero della Francesca's Mathematical Treatises: The "Trattato d'abaco" and "Libellus de quinque corporibus regularibus"* (Ravenna: Longo, 1977).

45. *"Nacque costui nel Borgo a S. Sepolcro . . . e chiamossi dal nome della madre 'della Francesca,' per essere ella restata gravida da lui quando il padre e suo marito mori, e per essere da lei alevato e aiutato a pervenire al grado che la sua buona sorte gli dava."* *Vite,* 1:488–89 ["Piero was born in Borgo a San Sepolcro . . . and he was called Della Francesca after the name of his mother, because she had been left pregnant with him at the death of her husband, his father, and because it was she who had brought him up and assisted him to attain to the rank that his good-fortune held out to him." *Lives,* 1:397].

46. Longhi, 174.

47. Battisti 2:224, doc. LX: *"'Monna Romana' donna di Benedetto di Pietro, mori odi 6 sepelita in Badia."* A document dated August 31, 1416, and preserved in the Archivio di Stato in Florence, records the sale of a property in order to obtain liquid funds for the dowery of *"Romana di Renzo di Carlo da Monterchi"*

(ibid., p. 217). Cf. Giorgio Mancini, "La madre di Piero della Francesca," *Bolletino d'arte* 1918, p. 61.

48. Vasari, "Vita di Piero della Francesca," *Vite*, 1:493 [*Lives*, 1:399].

CHAPTER 2

1. Battisti, 2:69ff.

2. Giorni, 6, n. 10. Remains of a fresco from the church of Santa Maria dei Servi now preserved in Borgo San Sepolcro doubtless predate that of Piero, and are in fact recorded in the archives, without any further conclusions being deducible from this, under the title *Madonna del Parto* (ibid., p. 5, n. 6).

3. Bertelli, 206, mentions in this connection the decor conceived by Andrea del Castagno for Villa Carducci in Legnaia, often evoked with regard to the *Madonna del Parto*.

4. The procedure in question consists of piercing holes at regular intervals along the lines of a full-scale drawing, which is then transferred to the *intonaco* by rubbing the paper with charcoal powder; hence the "pointed" appearance of some parts of the resulting lines. With regard to the fresco proper, Domenico Fiscali, who detached it from the wall in 1910, maintained that Piero, in order to prevent destruction of the intonaco, worked *a tempera* rather than *a buon fresco*. Although he finds it difficult to compare the painter's technique here with the one used in the Arezzo cycle, Guido Botticelli nonetheless observes that both works made use of a technique that he considers atypical: the use of binding agents foreign to contemporary *a fresco* practice (*Restauro*, 25).

5. Kenneth Clark, *Piero della Francesca* (London/New York: Phaedon Press, 1951), p. 37 [revised 1961 ed., p. 54]. By contrast, in her excellent little book on the *Madonna del Parto* Ingeborg Walter attaches great importance to Piero's having received the commission from the town where his mother was born, to the point of making his own the Chagall quip reported by Roberto Papini: "Isn't it life that should be reborn from the mother's breast, instead of death"? Cf. I. Walter, *Piero della Francesca Madonna del Parto. Ein Kunstwerk zwischen Politik und Devotion* (Frankfurt: Fischer Taschenbuch, 1992), p. 13. Along the same general lines, I mustn't neglect to mention the visit, cast as an initiatory scene, of Malraux to Monterchi imagined by Jean-François Lyotard, which sticks wholeheartedly to the legend—but with what splendid results! Such would have been the wish of Malraux himself, for whom only what was legendary was true (cf. J.-F. Lyotard, *Signed, Malraux* (1996), trans. Robert Harvey (Minneapolis: University of Minnesota Press, 1999), p. 302.

6. *Vite*, 1:497; *Lives*, 1:401.

7. One hopes that this aspect of the encounter with Piero's masterpiece will be preserved, despite the understandable concern of the authorities to exploit

fully, for economic as well as cultural reasons, a treasure of whose worth the inhabitants of Monterchi, doubtless after having long suspected it, as we shall see, are now fully aware. In 1944, Mario Salmi and Ugo Procacci learned this to their cost: having come to Monterchi to place the fresco in a safe place, they were prevented from doing so by the population, who had mistaken them for Germans in disguise. And in 1954 the town administrators refused to authorize the transport of Piero's work for presentation in the *Mostra dei quatro maestri del primo Rinascimento* (Giorni, 20–22).

8. How not to think here of the *Little Dancer* presented by Degas at the sixth Impressionist exhibition within what some at the time compared to a "beaker," but which only made more apparent the physiognomic traits that gave this sculpture the air of an "anatomical waxwork"?

9. *Restauro*, 12–13.

10. *"Nell'altare maggiore c'è come icona una immagine bellissima della gloriosa Vergine gestante, con due angeli della stessa bellezza"* (1605); *"una immagine bellissima della gloriosa Vergine partoriente"* (1618); *"un'icona abbastanza antica con l'immagine della beatissima Vergine gestante, dipinta nella parete da Pietro dei Franceschi pittore eccellente"* (1635), etc. (Giorni, 14–15).

11. Giorni (p. 13) accepts as characteristic in this regard the fact that mass was no longer celebrated on the altar whose "icon" was the *Madonna del Parto,* noting by way of justification Eugenio Battisti's support for this hypothesis.

12. *"Nel far ritorno a Monterchi passo a visitare la Chiesa del Campo Santo. Cantasi l'antifona della Beatissima Vergine sotto il titolo dell'Espettazione del parto e sua orazione, visito l'Altare che stava a dovere"* (Giorni: doc. XXXIX, p. 41).

13. Vincenzo Funghini, "Scoperta di un pregevole dipinto a Monterchi," *La Provincia di Arezzo,* Jan. 13, 1889; reprinted in *Arte et Storia,* 8, no. 1 (1889), p. 23 (Giorni, doc. XL, pp. 41–42).

14. *"Affresco. Raffigura la maternità di Maria . . . Al fresco . . . rappresenta la Madonna del Parto, attribuito a Pier della Francesca"* (Giorni, doc. XLI, pp. 42–43).

15. Battisti, 2:71.

16. See the iconography of the *Madonna del Parto* assembled by Thomas Martone in *Restauro,* pp. 103ff. Giovanni Pozzi thinks it is significant that Piero did not give the Madonna of Monterchi the symbolic girdle that signifies the pregnancy of the Virgin in Marian iconography, whereas the *Madonna della Misericordia* in Borgo exhibits this attribute, of which the town of Prato took pride in possessing a relic. Cf. Pozzi, p. 319.

17. "Now a great sign appeared in heaven: a woman, adorned with the sun, standing on the moon, and with the twelve stars on her head for a crown. She was pregnant, and in labor, crying aloud in the pangs of childbirth" (*Apocalypse,* 12:1–

2). The Apocalyptic Woman seems to symbolize not the Virgin but the People of God, of which Eve was the origin and who gave birth in pain, despite the reference shortly thereafter to the male child who was taken straight up to God and to his throne, whereas the woman escaped into the desert (ibid., 12:5–6, and the commentary that accompanies the text in the *Bible de Jérusalem* "Apocalypse," Paris, 1959, pp. 57–58). Cf. the *Madonna del Parto* in the Museo Bandini, in Fiesole, attributed to Nardo di Cione (*Restauro*, cat. no. 6, pp. 130–31). A connection between images of the Madonna del Parto and those of the Apocalyptic Woman was already posited by, among others, Millard Meiss, in *Painting in Florence and Siena After the Black Death: The Arts, Religion, and Society in the Mid-Fourteenth Century* (Princeton: Princeton University Press, 1951), p. 42, note 120.

18. Cf. Gilberto Freyre, *The Masters and the Slaves [Casa-grande e senzola]: A Study in the Development of Brazilian Civilization*, trans. Samuel Putnam (New York: Knopf, 1946), p. 30.

19. Battisti, 2:71.

20. "It would be somewhat impudent to pretend to assign greater or less importance to this or that mystery in the life of the most holy Virgin; however, without departing from the respect that is fitting, it seems permissible to think that in some fashion the nativity marks the culminating point of the life in this world of she upon whom the church has bestowed the title of 'mother of God.' Without diminishing in the least the other events that constitute the wondrous weft of this life, it seems that the Annunciation, the Visitation, and the Pentecost are but various aspects and consequences of the mystery of the Nativity. This is what the first Christian generations understood by giving this mystery a more pronounced attention." Dom Leclerq, "Maternité divine," in Fernand Cabrol, Henri Leclerq, et al., *Dictionnaire d'archéologie chrétienne et de liturgie*, 15 vols. (Paris: Letouzey et Ane, 1907–1953, vol. 10 (1932), 2, col. 1999–2000.

21. *"Die älteste und die brennendste Frage der jungen Menschheit . . . : die Frage nach der Herkunft der Kinder."* S. Freud, "Zur sexuellen Aufklärung der Kinder" (1907), *GW*, 8:175; "The Sexual Enlightenment of Children," *SE*, 9:135.

22. *"Die Rätselfrage . . . : woher die Kinder kommen."* S. Freud, "Über infantile Sexualtheorien" (1908), *GW*, 7, p. 175; "On the Sexual Theories of Children," *SE*, 9:212 [translation altered].

23. Ibid., *GW*, 7:175; *SE*, 9:213.

24. Ibid., *GW*, 7:175, 180–81; *SE*, 9:212, 218–19.

25. Freud/Leonardo, *GW*, 145; *SE*, 78.

26. "The core of his nature, and the secret of it, would appear to be that after his curiosity had been activated in infancy in the service of sexual interests he succeeded in sublimating the greater part of his libido into an urge for research." Freud/Leonardo, *GW*, 148; *SE*, 80–81.

27. *"Die grossen Fragen quälten, woher die Kinder kommen und was der Vater mit ihrer Enstehung su tun haben."* Freud/Leonardo, *GW,* 161; *SE,* 92.

28. Jacques Lacan, *Le Séminaire,* book 4, *La Relation d'objet* (Paris: Seuil, 1994), p. 421.

29. Freud/Leonardo, *GW,* 159; *SE,* 90.

30. The comparison between the Virgin and the vulture is found in a number of ancient sources, including the popular *Physiologus,* or bestiary, of the twelfth century (cf. T[erence] H[anbury] White, *The Book of Beasts, Being a Translation from a Latin Bestiary of the Twelfth Century,* London: Putnam, 1954, pp. 108–9).

31. Freud/Leonardo, *GW,* 159; *SE,* 90 [translation altered].

32. *Vite,* 499–500 ("Vita di Piero della Francesca"); *Lives,* 1:402. On the specifically literary dimension of Vasari's *Lives* as a work of *fiction,* cf. the previously mentioned trilogy of Paul Barolsky: *Michelangelo's Nose: A Myth and Its Maker* (University Park: Pennsylvania State University Press, 1990); *Why Mona Lisa Smiles and Other Tales by Vasari* (University Park: Pennsylvania State University Press, 1991); and *Giotto's Father and the Family of Vasari's "Lives"* (University Park: Pennsylvania State University Press, 1992).

33. S. Freud, "Über infantile Sexualtheorien," *GW,* 7:180; "On the Sexual Theories of Children," *SE,* 9:218.

34. Ibid., *GW,* 7:186; *SE,* 9:224.

CHAPTER 3

1. Freud, "Über infantile Sexualtheorien" (1908), *GW,* 7:188; "On the Sexual Theories of Children," *SE,* 9:226.

2. Long before Malinowski, Durkheim paid attention to the belief, widespread in Australian and Pacific societies, that the child is not the physiological offspring of its parents. That he based his argument on a supposed "intellectual laziness" of the "primitives" in an attempt to refute Tylor's hypothesis about the role of dreams in the origin of religious beliefs becomes especially interesting in a Freudian context: "Inevitably, such intellectual laziness is greatest in the primitive. This frail being, who must struggle so hard for his life against the forces that assail it, lacks the wherewithal for the luxury of speculation. He probably does not reflect unless he has to. It is therefore not easy to see what could have led him to make dreaming the topic of his meditations." Émile Durkheim, *The Elementary Forms of Religious Life* (1912), trans. Karen E. Fields (New York: Free Press, 1996), p. 55.

3. On the family books that the Florentines customarily kept between 1350 and 1530, cf. Klapisch-Zuber, *La Maison et le Nom.* [N.B.: Many, but not all, of the relevant essays from this volume are included in idem, *Women, Family,*

and Ritual in Renaissance Italy, trans. Lydia Cochrane (Chicago and London: University of Chicago Press, 1985).]

4. Ibid., p. 10 [N.B.: from introduction; not included in *Women, Family, and Ritual*].

5. Longhi, 173.

6. Alessandro della Vita, "Notizie sulla famiglia e sulla madre di Piero della Francesca," *Bolletino d'Arte,* Sept.–Oct. 1916, pp. 9–12; Battisti, 2:217ff; Bertelli, 12 and note 41. On the question of the name, cf. G. Gronau, "Piero della Francesca oder Piero dei Franceschi," *Repertorium für Kunstwissenschaft,* 1900, pp. 393–94, and the addendum to the entry "Piero dei Franceschi" in *Thieme-Beckers Künstlerlexicon,* vol. 12 (1916), pp. 289–94, as well as the documents assembled in Battisti, 2:218ff.

7. Battisti, 2:238, doc. CXCV.

8. On this point and the following one, cf. Klapisch-Zuber, op. cit. (see note 3), pp. 83–107, "Le nom 'refait'" ["The Name 'Remade'," *Women, Family, and Ritual,* op. cit. (see note 3), pp. 283–309].

9. Ibid., p. 10 [N.B.: from introduction; not in *Women, Family, and Ritual . . .*].

10. Battisti, 2:217–18; Klapisch-Zuber, op. cit. (see note 3), p. 106 [*Women, Family, and Ritual,* op. cit. (see note 3), p. 308].

11. Klapisch-Zuber, op. cit. (see note 3), p. 83 [*Women, Family, and Ritual,* op. cit. (see note 3), p. 283–84].

12. Millard Meiss, *Painting in Florence and Siena after the Black Death: The Arts, Religion, and Society in the Mid-Fourteenth Century* (Princeton: Princeton University Press, 1951)

13. One cannot help but be struck in this connection by the strange determination with which some of the best authors set out to deny any relationship between the *Madonna del Parto* and, if not Piero's mother, then at least his maternal line. Such as Eugenio Battisti, for whom all family ties and relationships are excluded, despite the rantings of certain ostensible descendants of the Franceschi family, since (1) the painter did not own any property in Monterchi and (2) contrary to the fable invented by Vasari, his mother was not a "Francesca da Monterchi." A Francesca, without any doubt; but a Romana? The denial becomes a Freudian slip when Battisti goes so far as to credit Vasari with the hypothesis of a mother born in Monterchi, whereas the author of the *Lives* limited himself to saying that Piero was raised by his mother, born della Francesca, his father having died before his birth, without making any allusion to the country of origin that was well and truly Monna Romana's, any more than to the fresco that Piero would paint there.

14. Cf. Matthew 1:16: "And Jacob was the father of Joseph called the

husband of Mary; of her was born Jesus who is called Christ." And Luke 3:23: "When he started to teach, Jesus was about thirty years old, being the son, as it was thought, of Joseph."

15. Marina Warner, *Alone of All Her Sex: The Myth and Cult of the Virgin Mary* (New York: Vintage Books, 1976), p. 20; cf. Edmund Leach, "Virgin Birth," in *Genesis as Myth and Other Essays* (London: Jonathan Cape, 1969), pp. 85–112 and 117–22 (notes). Even today, the commentary in the French edition of the Jerusalem Bible does not shy away from invoking the sociological model while keeping that of the Church Fathers in reserve, striking a balance (at the risk confusing them) between the two lineages, paternal and maternal, and likewise between the two lines of descent, human and divine, as church tradition has constantly maintained: "Both lists lead to Joseph, who is only the legal father of Jesus: in the view of the ancients, legal paternity (through adoption, levirate, etc.) sufficed to confer all hereditary rights, here those of the Davidic lineage. That does not preclude Mary herself belonging to this lineage, although the gospels do not say this."

16. Cf. Klapisch-Zuber, op. cit. (see note 3), pp. 151–83 ["Zacharias, or the Ousted Father: Nuptial Rites in Tuscany Between Giotto and the Council of Trent," *Women, Family, and Ritual . . .* , op. cit. (see note 3), pp. 178–212.

17. Warner, op. cit. (see note 15), p. 33.

18. Cf., among others, the famous passages on the "true kinsmen of Jesus" in Matthew 12:46–50, Luke 8:19–21, and Mark 3:31–35.

19. Freud/Leonardo, *GW,* 152; *SE,* 84 [N.B.: bracketed phrase in *SE*].

20. Freud, "Der Moses des Michelangelos" (1914), *GW,* 10:172–201; "The Moses of Michelangelo," *SE,* 13:211–38. I take the liberty of referring the reader to my discussion of this text in "Le gardien de l'interprétation," *Tel Quel,* no. 4 (winter 1971), pp. 70–84; and no. 45 (spring 1971), pp. 82–96.

21. Their time [*Zeit*], not their "context," as we would more likely say today. Cf. Walter Benjamin, "Literary History and the Study of Literature" (1931), trans. Rodney Livingstone, in idem, *Selected Writings,* ed. Michael W. Jennings, Howard Eiland, and Gary Smith, 4 vols. (Cambridge, Mass./London: Belknap Press of Harvard University, 1997–[in progress]), vol. 2 (1999), p. 464 [translation altered].

CHAPTER 4

1. For an erudite critique of the fantasy of a female monotheism corresponding to the cult of the Great Goddess, Mother of the gods, as well as of the myth conducive to viewing the Virgin Mary as heir to the great goddesses of antiquity, cf. Philippe Borgeaud, *La Mère des dieux. De Cybèle à la Vierge Marie* (Paris: Seuil, 1996).

2. Pozzi, 317.

3. Maurizio Calvesi, "Il vero significato di un capolavoro enigmatico. Nel grembo dell'arca," in *Speciale Piero. Studi e riscoperte, Art dossier,* no. 33 (Mar. 1989), pp. 16–20.

4. Pozzi, 308–9.

5. Pozzi, 293, 312.

6. "Conception and gestation were placed under the protection of Mary since Ephesus had proclaimed her 'theotokos'" (Pozzi, 317).

7. Teodoro Studita, *Antirrheticus,* 3:2–3, cited in Pozzi, 311.

8. "But why this grand silence, Mary?—I am discovering it, Magdalene.— What are you talking about?—About the one who speaks and myself who expresses it.—About yourself? Outside yourself?—About myself who receives this birth.—You receive, you do not give?—Yes I gave to vision.—I don't see, Mary—Magdalene, you don't see that this is in my body?" Jean-Luc Godard, "Vu par le boeuf et l'âne" (1984), in *Jean-Luc Godard par Jean-Luc Godard,* ed. Alain Bergala (Paris: Éditions d'Étoile, 1985), p. 588.

9. Dominique Paini, "La bonne distance," *Art Press,* unnumbered issue, "Spécial Godard," Dec. 1984. On the question of figurability as posed in *Le Chef-d'oeuvre inconnu,* see my introduction to *Fenêtre cadmium jaune* (Paris: Seuil, 1984), pp. 11–46, "Les dessous de la peinture."

10. The *Mérode Altarpiece* is an exception to the rule, even though Joseph is relegated there to a side panel, apart from the central scene, occupied as he is with a task enigmatic for a carpenter. In a justly celebrated article, Meyer Schapiro claims to demonstrate that the introduction of Joseph was connected to the development of the cult of this saint at the end of the fourteenth century, in the guise of guardian of the mystery of the Incarnation, and that the mousetrap he is making is a condensation of diabolical and erotic symbols as well as their repression: the trap being at once a female object and a means of repressing sexual temptation. Cf. M. Schapiro, "'Muscipula Diaboli': The Symbolism of the Mérode Altarpiece" (1945), in *Selected Papers III: Late Antique, Early Christian, and Medieval Art* (New York: Braziller, 1979), pp. 1–19.

11. Cf. Charles Daremberg and Edmond Saglio, *Dictionnaire des antiquités grecques et romaines,* 5 vols. (Paris: Hachette, 1877–1919), vol. 5, p. 675, entry "velum."

12. Pliny the Elder, *Natural History,* book 35, chap. 35; trans. H. Rackham (Loeb Classical Library; Cambridge, Mass.: Harvard University Press, 1984), vol. 9, pp. 304–5.

13. "*Similitudo tabernaculi quod ostendimus vobis*": Exodus 25:9, cited in Pozzi, 321.

14. Cf. Vern L. Bullough, "Medieval Medical and Scientific Views of

Women," *Viator,* 4 (1973), pp. 487–93. In the matter of generation, Montaigne still deferred to the Aristotelian tradition that saw form as an exclusive contribution of the man, the woman being incapable of this: "And as we see that women, all alone, produce mere shapeless masses and lumps of flesh, but that to create a good and natural offspring they must be made fertile with a different kind of seed" (*Essais,* book 1, chap. 8, "Of Idleness") [*The Complete Essays of Montaigne,* trans. Donald M. Frame (Stanford, Calif.: Stanford University Press, 1958), pp. 20–21]. Transposed into the esthetic order, the pairing on the one hand of form with masculinity and on the other hand of the unformed with femininity would prove remarkably tenacious; Karl Scheffer, on the eve of World War I, was not the last person to defend the idea that woman is unfit for giving form (*Die Frau und die Kunst. Eine Studie* [Berlin, 1908]).

15. Millard Meiss, "The Madonna of Humility," *Art Bulletin,* 18 (1936), pp. 435–64; reprinted in idem, *Painting in Florence and Siena After the Black Death: The Arts, Religion, and Society in the Mid-Fourteenth Century* (Princeton: Princeton University Press, 1951), pp. 132–56.

16. If we are to believe the ground plan traced by Thomas Martone (*Convegno,* p. 61, pl. 24), the Virgin is actually standing on the threshold of the tent, and not inside it. As Battisti observes, this description, which is premised on the notion (debatable at best) of "perspectival realism," is contradicted, on the phenomenological register, by the position of the feet of the two angels: they are clearly further forward than those of the Virgin ("Alcuni accenni al dibattito pierfrancescano in corso," ibid., p. 191).

Note added to the proofs of the French edition: If we try, by contrast, to reconstruct the drawing of the two symmetrical pockets of folds exhibited by these same angels on a level with their belts, and which are partly hidden by their lowered arms, we cannot but see in them an implicit allusion to the gynecological discussions about the Virgin—even if we take them to be "imbecilic quibbles" (Françoise Dolto, interviewed by Gérard Séverin, *The Jesus of Psychoanalysis: A Freudian Interpretation of the Gospel,* trans. Helen R. Lane, Garden City, N.Y.: Doubleday, 1979, p. 26). According to Vasari, Piero was "much given to making models in clay, on which he spread wet draperies with an infinity of folds, in order to make use of them for drawing" (Vasari, 1:402). Concerning this "curiously arranged and rather confusing drapery" (as Freud says about the robe of Mary, itself traversed by an arm that partly obscures it, in the painting by Leonardo da Vinci now in the Louvre, *Virgin and Child with Saint Anne* [Freud/Leonardo, *SE,* 115; note added in 1919]), which contrasts unmistakably with the perfectly regular folds of the Virgin's robe, it is hard to see how it could have resulted from such an imitation. Instead of folds, these circumvolutions are more evocative of the ear, or of internal organs of ill-defined aspect, visceral, genital, or cardiac.

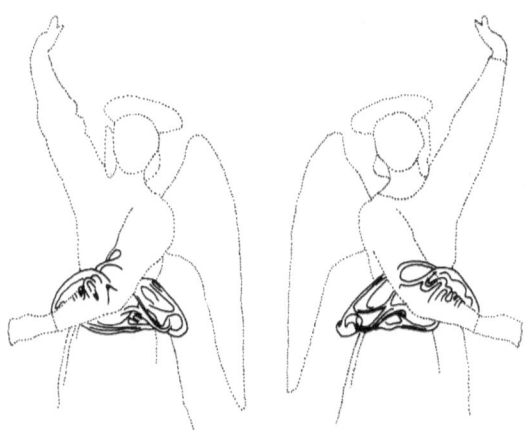

Madonna del Parto, detail of the angels' robes.

The gnosis urging that the Virgin was impregnated through the ear would be echoed here by the "cloacal" childhood sexual theory, according to which infants are evacuated like pieces of excrement—which would solve the problem of the origin of babies, insofar as it holds them to be conceived by eating and delivered into the world by the intestines (Freud/Leonardo, *SE,* 79; S. Freud, "On the Sexual Theories of Children," *SE,* 9:219). And echoed as well as by the oft-noted relation between the heart and the uterus: that is, something very like the vulture whose contours the good pastor Pfister thought he discerned in the folds of the robe of Leonardo's Virgin, similar to an "unconscious picture-puzzle" (*als unbewusstes Vexierbild;* Freud/Leonardo, *GW,* 187; *SE,* 115), which of course cannot be accepted without reservations. Herself referring to Freud's work on childhood sexual theories, Caroline Walker Bynum does not overlook the fascination of Guerric, abbot of the Cistercian monastery of Igny († ca. 1157), with images of pregnancy and of the uterus; in addition to speaking of the soul hiding itself in the wounds and heart of Christ, he explicitly associates the heart with the uterus, going so far as to produce a bizarre description of the soul as a child incorporated into the bowels of God the Father: "He draws them [the wretched] into his very bowels and makes them his members (*in ipsa sua eos viscer trahit suisque inserit membris*)" Cf. Guerric of Igny, "Second Sermon for Lent," in idem, *Sermons,* ed. John Morson and Hilary Costello, 2 vols. (Paris: Éditions du Cerf, 1970–1973), vol. 2, pp. 30–31; as cited by Bynum, *Jesus as Mother: Studies in the Spirituality of the High Middle Ages* (Berkeley: University of California Press, 1982), p. 121.

17. *"Ma sopra ogni altra considerazione e d'ingegno e d'arte, è lo avere dipinto e la notte et un Angelo in iscorto che, venendo a capo all'ingiù a portare il seno della vittoria a Costantino che dorme in un padiglione guardato da un cameriere e da alcuni armati oscurati dalle notte, con la stessa luce sua illumina il padiglione, gl'armati e tutti i dintorni, con grandissima discrezione. . . . Il che avendo egli fatto benissimo, ha dato cagione ai moderni di seguitarlo e di venire a quel grado sommo, dove si veggiono ne'tempi nostri le cose"* (*Vite,* 496 ["But above every other consideration, whether of imagination or of art, is his painting of Night, with an angel in foreshortening who is flying with his head downwards, bringing the sign of victory to Constantine, who is sleeping in a pavilion, guarded by a chamberlain and some men-at-arms who are seen dimly through the darkness of the night; and with his own light the angel illuminates the pavilion, the men-at-arms, and all the surroundings. This is done with very great thought . . . which he did so well that he enabled the moderns to attain, by following him, to that supreme perfection wherein art is seen in our own time"; *Lives,* 1:400]).

18. *Convegno,* figs. 97–100.

19. *Book of James,* 10–11; cf. *Évangiles apocryphes,* ed. France Queré (Paris, 1983), pp. 75–76.

20. Bernardo de'Busti (a preacher contemporary with Piero), *Mariale Sermo 6,* cited in Pozzi, 301.

21. *Restauro,* cat. 1, p. 121. In the Baroque period, painters and sculptors did not hesitate to inscribe the monogram of Christ on the prominent belly of the Virgin (ibid., fig. 20, p. 117).

22. Pozzi, 316.

23. Syriac ms., BN [N.B.: Bibliotheque national de France; "BN" is part of call number in the manuscript department.] 341, fol. 118. Cf. *Mémoires et monuments publiés par l'Académie des inscriptions et belles-lettres* (Paris, E. Leroux), vol. 17, pl. V, n. 17; Cabrol, Leclerq, et al., *Dictionnaire d'archéologie chrétienne et de liturgie,* vol. 10 (1932), 2, entry "Marie, mère de Dieu," col. 2014.

24. G. H. Luquet, "Représentation par transparence de la grossesse dans l'art chrétien," *Revue archéologique,* 19 (Jan.–June 1924), pp. 137–49.

25. Cf. Yves Congar, "Modèle monastique et modèle sacerdotal en Occident de Grégoire VII (1073–1085) à Innocent III (1198)," in *Études de civilisation médiévale IXe–XIIe siècles: Mélanges offerts à Edmond-René Labande* (Poitiers: C.É.S.C.M., 1973), p. 159; cited by C. Bynum, op. cit. (see note 16), p. 11.

26. Pozzi, 320.

27. Hence images that present the infant Jesus, already fully formed, borne by golden rays extending from the angel or the dove to the Virgin. Cf. Pozzi, 275; see also Daniel Arasse, "Annonciation/Énonciation. Remarques sur un énoncé pictural au Quattrocento," *Versus. Quaderni di studi semiotici,* 37 (1984),

pp. 3–17; and Louis Marin, "Annonciations toscanes," in *Opacité de la peinture. Essais sur la représentation au Quattrocento* (Paris: Usher, 1989), pp. 125–63.
28. Cf. note 16.
29. Reproduced in the exhibition catalogue *Andrea Mantegna*, ed. Jane Martineau, London and New York, 1992, cat. no. 16, pp. 158–60.
30. Longhi, 23, 35, 43.

CHAPTER 5

1. "*El quale reputo essere una finestra aperta per donde io miri quello che quivi sarà dipinto*": Leon Battista Alberti, *Della Pittura*, book I, 19, ed. Luigi Mallé (Florence: Sansoni, 1950), p. 70. Despite Jean-Louis Schefer's remarkable French translation of *De Pictura*, Alberti's original Latin version (Paris, 1992), I will refer primarily to the Italian text written in 1436, a year after the Latin one, which at many points I find more concrete and vivid than the initial text (English: *On Painting*, trans. from the Latin by Cecil Grayson (London/New York: Penguin, 1991), p. 54).
2. Latin "*quoniam picturam diximus esser intercisionem pyramidis*"; Italian "*poi che dicemmo la pittura essere intercissione della pirramide.*" Ibid. (Mallé ed.), book I, 12, p. 65; Schefer ed., p. 102 (*On Painting*, p. 48).
3. "*In questa superficia si representino le forme delle cose vedute*"; ibid.
4. Ibid. (Mallé ed.), book I, 12, p. 65; Schefer ed., p. 103 (*On Painting*, p. 48).
5. Ibid. Five centuries later, Fox Talbot would entitle the first book with photographic illustrations, in which he sought to demonstrate the medium's ability to capture all of light's nuances, *The Pencil of Nature* (London, 1844).
6. "*Quadrangulum rectorum angulorum inscribo, quod quidem mihi pro aperta finestra est ex qua historia contueatur*"; L.-B. Alberti, op. cit. (Schefer ed.), book I, 19, pp. 114–15 (*On Painting*, p. 54 [translation altered]).
7. "*De hac igitur, caeteris omissis referam quid ipse dum pingo eficiam*"; "*Qui solo, lassate l'altre cose, diro quello fo io quando dipingo*"; Alberti, op. cit. (Schefer ed.), pp. 114–15; Mallé ed., p. 70 (*On Painting*, p. 54).
8. Longhi, 25.
9. Pascal Bonitzer, *Décadrages, Peinture et cinéma* (Paris, 1985), p. 63.
10. "*La linea che giace nel quadrangolo*": Alberti, op. cit.
11. "*La prima parte è il vedere, cioè l'ochio . . . , da quale non intendo tractare se non quanto fie necessario a la pictura. Dunque dico l'ochio essere la prima parte, perchè gli è quello in cui s'apresentano tucte le cose vedute socto diversi angoli*"; Piero della Francesca, *De prospectiva pingendi*, ed. Nicco Fasola (Florence: Sansoni, 1942; new ed. 1984), p. 64.
12. "*La quinta [parte] è uno termine nel quale l'occhio descrive co'suoi raggi le cose proportionalmente et posse in quello giudicare la loro mesura; se non fusse*

termine non si potra intendere quanto le cose degradassaro, si che non se porieno dimostrare"; ibid., pp. 64–65.

13. "*Oltra di questo è necessario sapere lineare in propria form sopra il piano tucte le cose che l'omo intende fare*"; ibid., p. 65.

14. Longhi, 28 [translation altered]. The masonry metaphor, which comes down to assimilating the *Flagellation* to an opaque wall of paint, literally excludes any idea of a transparent window piercing the wall.

15. "*Verbi gratia sia A. l'ochio*"; Piero della Francesca, op. cit. (see note 11), p. 66.

16. Ibid., book I, proposition XXX, pp. 96–99. Cf. H. Damisch, *The Origin of Perspective* (1987), trans. John Goodman (Cambridge, Mass.: MIT Press, 1994), pp. 346–51.

17. Cf. *The Origin of Perspective*, op. cit. (see previous note), pp. 344–52.

18. Cf. pertinent discussion in next chapter.

CHAPTER 6

1. As Heidegger stated in his intervention in Fink's seminar on Heraclitus: "Standing open is not something like an open window or like a passageway. The standing open of humans to things does not mean that there is a hole through which humans see." Cf. M. Heidegger and Eugen Fink, *Heraclitus Seminar, 1966–67*, trans. Charles H. Seibert (University: University of Alabama Press, 1979), p. 125.

2. Cf. Damisch, *The Origin of Perspective*, pp. 264–67 and 427–28.

3. Freud, "Aus der Geschichte einer infantilen Neurose," *GW*, 12:55; "From the History of an Infantile Neurosis," *SE*, 17:29.

4. Dominique Paini, "La bonne distance," *Art Press*, unnumbered issue, "Spécial Godard," Dec. 1984.

5. Freud, "Aus der Geschichte . . . ," op. cit. (see note 3), *GW*, 12:96; "From the History . . . , *SE*, 17:65.

6. Ibid.

7. Ibid., *GW*, 12:93; *SE*, 17:62.

8. In the same sense, but in a wholly different context, cf. Bynum, *Jesus as Mother*, p. 167.

9. Cf. J. Lacan, *Le Séminaire*, book 4, *La Relation d'objet* (Paris: Seuil, 1994), pp. 40–52. Remember that, according to Freud, the first infantile sexual theory stems from a neglect of the differences between the sexes. "It consists in *attributing to everyone, including females, the possession of a penis*, such as the boy knows from his own body" (Freud, "Über infantile Sexualtheorien," *GW*, 7:177; "On the Sexual Theories of Children," *SE*, 9:215). On the question of the mother as the first love object for both sexes, and the related question of the

two aspects, masculine and feminine, of the Oedipus complex, see the beautiful book by Marie-Christine Hamon, *Why Do Women Love Men and Not Their Mothers? Freud and Femininity* (1992) trans. Susan Fairfield (New York: Other Press, 2000), which offers a very new take on Freud's belatedly (*nachträglich*) evolving conception of femininity, a project that he undertook through a sustained dialogue with his female students. Proof, if need be, that the "return to Freud" remains more current than ever.

10. J. Lacan, op. cit. (see previous note), p. 34.

11. Adducing Freud's note on the *Santa Anna Metterza* (the "tripartite Saint Anne" by Leonardo), André Green rightly contrasts divine Trinities, which allow the mother no place, with human Trinities, which do without the Father; cf. André Green, *Révélations de l'inachèvement. A propos du carton de Londres de Léonard de Vinci* (Paris: Flammarion, 1992).

12. Pozzi, 315.

13. J. Lacan, op. cit. (see note 9), p. 155.

14. Ibid., p. 156. A "nothing," by the way, that might well have something to do, if not *à voir*, with this other "nothing" that psychoanalysis has had to say, by way of Freud, about beauty, which he reattached to the sphere of sexual feelings, and whose assignation would proceed from a displacement from the sphere of the genital organs, never or rarely considered beautiful, onto "secondary" sexual traits, the "attractions." The question of beauty henceforth being related to that of the phallus and presenting an imaginary as well as a symbolic dimension, being itself linked to the beyond toward which this nothing signals. Cf., on this point, the first chapter of my *The Judgment of Paris* (1992), trans. John Goodman (Chicago: The University of Chicago Press, 1996), pp. 1–12.

15. Longhi: 19–24.

16. J. Lacan, op. cit. (see note 9), p. 156.

17. Cf. Pozzi: 305–06.

18. Cf. H. Damisch, *The Origin of Perspective*, op. cit. (see note 2), pp. 119–21.

19. The configuration devised by Piero is strikingly like the one implied by an adaptation of the camera obscura proposed by Charles Chevalier (1819). That is, a complex configuration, but one that, through the detour of a prism acting like a mirror, aims to do just what Alberti's *velum* does: "Often one projects images directly onto the sheet of paper and the draftsman has only to follow their outlines. To this end, a perfectly reflective prism is placed toward the upper part of a tube supported by three legs. A black drape forms something like a small tent, below which the draftsman places himself such that the exterior light will not prevent him from distinguishing clearly the image projected onto the screen. This screen consists of a sheet of paper placed on an adjustable table that can be raised or lowered to achieve focus. The rays that traverse the prism are

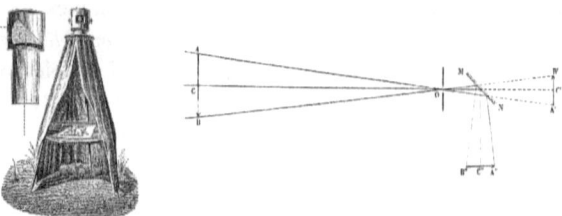

Adaptation of the darkroom of the completely reflective prism and schema showing the path of the light rays, after Augustin Bouton and J.-Ch. D'Almeida, *Cours élémentaire de physique*, 2nd edition, Paris, Dunod, 1863, p. 725.

reflected and draw the image on the sheet of paper." Augustin Bouton and J.-Ch. D'Almeida, *Cours élémentaire de physique*, 2nd ed. (Paris: Dunod, 1863), p. 725.

The difference—a significant one—is linked, as shown in the diagram in the above illustration, to the initially horizontal motion of the rays reflected in the mirror indicated by the line MN, whereas in the *Madonna del Parto* the lines (which can scarcely be said to recede) converge on the vertical. I thank my friend Michel Frizot for having made me aware of this document.

I note further that, in the French lexicon of photography, an *obturateur* (shutter) is a device (sometimes an *obturateur à rideau* [curtain shutter]) whereby light traversing the lens hits the sensitized surface at the intended moment, the (antinomic) function of the device being, paradoxically, to allow light to pass through the very hole that it normally blocks. According to the *Petit Robert*, the French word also designates, in human anatomy, the membranes and muscles serving to stop up the *trou sous-pubien* [thyroid foramen], itself also called an *obturateur* [obturator].

20. Henri Focillon, *Piero della Francesca* (Paris: A. Colin, 1952), p. 48.

21. H. Lacan, op. cit. (see note 9), p. 157.

22. *Republic*, book 2, 381 b–c.

23. S. Freud, "Konstruktionen in der Analyse" (1937), *GW*, 16:44; "Constructions in Analysis," *SE*, 23:258.

24. Ibid., *GW*, 16:46–47; *SE*, 23:260.

25. Ibid.

26. Cf. pertinent discussion in Chapter 2.

27. Freud, "Konstruktionen . . . ," op. cit. (see note 23), *GW*, 16:47; *SE*, 23:260.

28. "*Die analytische Arbeit aus zwei ganz verschiedenen Stücken besteht, dass sie sich auf zwei gesonderten Schauplätzen vollzieht, an zwei Personen vor sich geht,*

von denen jedem eine andere Aufgabe zugewiesen ist"—"The work of analysis consists of two quite different portions/plays, which are carried out in two separate arenas and involve two people, to each of whom a distinct task is assigned"; ibid., *GW,* 16:44–45; *SE,* 23:258 [translation altered]. Winnicott translated this idea of a double arena into ludic terms: the intersection or overlapping of two distinct areas of playing; cf. D. W. Winnicott, *Playing and Reality* (London and New York: Routledge, 1982), pp. 38–53. First published in 1971.

29. Freud, "Konstruktionen . . . ," op. cit. (see note 23), *GW,* 16:45; "Constructions . . . ," *SE,* 23:258–259.

30. Freud/Leonardo, *GW,* 151; *SE,* 83 (in footnote added in 1919).

31. Cf. pertinent discussion toward the end of Chapter 3.

32. "The essence of it is that there is not only *method* in madness, as the poet has already perceived, but also a fragment of *historical truth* (*ein Stück historischer Wahrheit*)"; Freud, "Konstruktionen . . . ," op. cit. (see note 23), *GW,* 16:54; "Constructions . . . ," *SE,* 23:267.

33. One knows the story, recounted in the apocryphal *Book of James,* of Salome's hand having been burned because she tried to verify, *de tactu,* the virginity of the "mother of God." Cf. *Évangiles apocryphes,* ed. France Queré (Paris, 1983), p. 81. For his part, the doctor in Godard's *Je vous salue Marie* doesn't pull his punches [*n'y va de main morte*].

34. J. Lacan, op. cit. (see note 9), p. 157.

35. "Of the physician's point of view I can only declare that in a case of this kind he must behave as 'timelessly' [*ebenso 'zeitlos'*] as the unconscious itself, if he wishes to learn anything or achieve anything." Freud, "Aus der Geschichte . . . ," op. cit. (see note 3), *GW,* 12:33; *SE,* 17:10.

36. J. Lacan, op. cit. (see note 9), p. 48.

37. "*Dico que la prospectiva sona nel nome suo commo dire cose vedute da lungi, rapresentate socto certi dati termini con proportione, secondo le distantie loro.*" Piero della Francesca, *De prospectiva pingendi,* p. 128.

38. Cf. Damisch, *The Judgment of Paris,* op. cit. (see note 14), pp. 107–98 [N.B.: Damisch's subtitle for this book, "*iconologie analytique 1,*" was excised from the English-language edition.—trans.].

39. "If the unconscious arises where 'it' doesn't think (*Wo es war, soll Ich Werden*—'where it/Id was, I/Ego shall be'), thinking the unconscious always entails the risk of letting some of its meaning escape: 'Where "it" was, there was no thinking it.'" M.-C. Hamon, op. cit. (see note 9), p. 20 [translation altered].

40. "*La natura è piena d'infinite ragioni che non furono mai in isperienza.*" Leonardo da Vinci, cited by Freud in the last lines of "Leonardo da Vinci and a Memory of His Childhood," Freud/Leonardo, *GW,* 211; *SE,* 137 [translation altered].

Cultural Memory | *in the Present*

Asja Szafraniec, *Beckett, Derrida, and the Event of Literature*

Alison Ross, *The Aesthetic Paths of Philosophy: Presentation in Kant, Heidegger, Lacoue-Labarthe, and Nancy*

Gerhard Richter, *Thought-Images: Frankfurt School Writers' Reflections from Damaged Life*

Bella Brodzki, *Can These Bones Live? Translation, Survival, and Cultural Memory*

Rodolphe Gasché, *The Honor of Thinking: Critique, Theory, Philosophy*

Brigitte Peucker, *The Material Image: Art and the Real in Film*

Natalie Melas, *All the Difference in the World: Postcoloniality and the Ends of Comparison*

Jonathan Culler, *The Literary in Theory*

Michael G. Levine, *The Belated Witness: Literature, Testimony, and the Question of Holocaust Survival*

Jennifer A. Jordan, *Structures of Memory: Understanding German Change in Berlin and Beyond*

Christoph Menke, *Reflections of Equality*

Marlène Zarader, *The Unthought Debt: Heidegger and the Hebraic Heritage*

Jan Assmann, *Religion and Cultural Memory: Ten Studies*

David Scott and Charles Hirschkind, *Powers of the Secular Modern: Talal Asad and His Interlocutors*

Gyanendra Pandey, *Routine Violence: Nations, Fragments, Histories*

James Siegel, *Naming the Witch*

J. M. Bernstein, *Against Voluptuous Bodies: Late Modernism and the Meaning of Painting*

Theodore W. Jennings, Jr., *Reading Derrida / Thinking Paul: On Justice*

Richard Rorty and Eduardo Mendieta, *Take Care of Freedom and Truth Will Take Care of Itself: Interviews with Richard Rorty*

Jacques Derrida, *Paper Machine*

Renaud Barbaras, *Desire and Distance: Introduction to a Phenomenology of Perception*

Jill Bennett, *Empathic Vision: Affect, Trauma, and Contemporary Art*

Ban Wang, *Illuminations from the Past: Trauma, Memory, and History in Modern China*

James Phillips, *Heidegger's Volk: Between National Socialism and Poetry*

Frank Ankersmit, *Sublime Historical Experience*

István Rév, *Retroactive Justice: Prehistory of Post-Communism*

Paola Marrati, *Genesis and Trace: Derrida Reading Husserl and Heidegger*

Krzysztof Ziarek, *The Force of Art*

Marie-José Mondzain, *Image, Icon, Economy: The Byzantine Origins of the Contemporary Imaginary*

Cecilia Sjöholm, *The Antigone Complex: Ethics and the Invention of Feminine Desire*

Jacques Derrida and Elisabeth Roudinesco, *For What Tomorrow . . . : A Dialogue*

Elisabeth Weber, *Questioning Judaism: Interviews by Elisabeth Weber*

Jacques Derrida and Catherine Malabou, *Counterpath: Traveling with Jacques Derrida*

Martin Seel, *Aesthetics of Appearing*

Nanette Salomon, *Shifting Priorities: Gender and Genre in Seventeenth-Century Dutch Painting*

Jacob Taubes, *The Political Theology of Paul*

Jean-Luc Marion, *The Crossing of the Visible*

Eric Michaud, *The Cult of Art in Nazi Germany*

Anne Freadman, *The Machinery of Talk: Charles Peirce and the Sign Hypothesis*

Stanley Cavell, *Emerson's Transcendental Etudes*

Stuart McLean, *The Event and Its Terrors: Ireland, Famine, Modernity*

Beate Rössler, ed., *Privacies: Philosophical Evaluations*

Bernard Faure, *Double Exposure: Cutting Across Buddhist and Western Discourses*

Alessia Ricciardi, *The Ends of Mourning: Psychoanalysis, Literature, Film*

Alain Badiou, *Saint Paul: The Foundation of Universalism*

Gil Anidjar, *The Jew, the Arab: A History of the Enemy*

Jonathan Culler and Kevin Lamb, eds., *Just Being Difficult? Academic Writing in the Public Arena*

Jean-Luc Nancy, *A Finite Thinking*, edited by Simon Sparks

Theodor W. Adorno, *Can One Live after Auschwitz? A Philosophical Reader*, edited by Rolf Tiedemann

Patricia Pisters, *The Matrix of Visual Culture: Working with Deleuze in Film Theory*

Andreas Huyssen, *Present Pasts: Urban Palimpsests and the Politics of Memory*

Talal Asad, *Formations of the Secular: Christianity, Islam, Modernity*

Dorothea von Mücke, *The Rise of the Fantastic Tale*

Marc Redfield, *The Politics of Aesthetics: Nationalism, Gender, Romanticism*

Emmanuel Levinas, *On Escape*

Dan Zahavi, *Husserl's Phenomenology*

Rodolphe Gasché, *The Idea of Form: Rethinking Kant's Aesthetics*

Michael Naas, *Taking on the Tradition: Jacques Derrida and the Legacies of Deconstruction*

Herlinde Pauer-Studer, ed., *Constructions of Practical Reason: Interviews on Moral and Political Philosophy*

Jean-Luc Marion, *Being Given That: Toward a Phenomenology of Givenness*

Theodor W. Adorno and Max Horkheimer, *Dialectic of Enlightenment*

Ian Balfour, *The Rhetoric of Romantic Prophecy*

Martin Stokhof, *World and Life as One: Ethics and Ontology in Wittgenstein's Early Thought*

Gianni Vattimo, *Nietzsche: An Introduction*

Jacques Derrida, *Negotiations: Interventions and Interviews, 1971–1998*, ed. Elizabeth Rottenberg

Brett Levinson, *The Ends of Literature: The Latin American "Boom" in the Neoliberal Marketplace*

Timothy J. Reiss, *Against Autonomy: Cultural Instruments, Mutualities, and the Fictive Imagination*

Hent de Vries and Samuel Weber, eds., *Religion and Media*

Niklas Luhmann, *Theories of Distinction: Re-Describing the Descriptions of Modernity*, ed. and introd. William Rasch

Johannes Fabian, *Anthropology with an Attitude: Critical Essays*

Michel Henry, *I Am the Truth: Toward a Philosophy of Christianity*

Gil Anidjar, *"Our Place in Al-Andalus": Kabbalah, Philosophy, Literature in Arab-Jewish Letters*

Hélène Cixous and Jacques Derrida, *Veils*

F. R. Ankersmit, *Historical Representation*

F. R. Ankersmit, *Political Representation*

Elissa Marder, *Dead Time: Temporal Disorders in the Wake of Modernity (Baudelaire and Flaubert)*

Reinhart Koselleck, *The Practice of Conceptual History: Timing History, Spacing Concepts*

Niklas Luhmann, *The Reality of the Mass Media*

Hubert Damisch, *A Theory of /Cloud/: Toward a History of Painting*

Jean-Luc Nancy, *The Speculative Remark: (One of Hegel's bon mots)*

Jean-François Lyotard, *Soundproof Room: Malraux's Anti-Aesthetics*

Jan Patočka, *Plato and Europe*

Hubert Damisch, *Skyline: The Narcissistic City*

Isabel Hoving, *In Praise of New Travelers: Reading Caribbean Migrant Women Writers*

Richard Rand, ed., *Futures: Of Jacques Derrida*

William Rasch, *Niklas Luhmann's Modernity: The Paradoxes of Differentiation*

Jacques Derrida and Anne Dufourmantelle, *Of Hospitality*

Jean-François Lyotard, *The Confession of Augustine*

Kaja Silverman, *World Spectators*

Samuel Weber, *Institution and Interpretation: Expanded Edition*

Jeffrey S. Librett, *The Rhetoric of Cultural Dialogue: Jews and Germans in the Epoch of Emancipation*

Ulrich Baer, *Remnants of Song: Trauma and the Experience of Modernity in Charles Baudelaire and Paul Celan*

Samuel C. Wheeler III, *Deconstruction as Analytic Philosophy*

David S. Ferris, *Silent Urns: Romanticism, Hellenism, Modernity*

Rodolphe Gasché, *Of Minimal Things: Studies on the Notion of Relation*

Sarah Winter, *Freud and the Institution of Psychoanalytic Knowledge*

Samuel Weber, *The Legend of Freud: Expanded Edition*

Aris Fioretos, ed., *The Solid Letter: Readings of Friedrich Hölderlin*

J. Hillis Miller / Manuel Asensi, *Black Holes / J. Hillis Miller; or, Boustrophedonic Reading*

Miryam Sas, *Fault Lines: Cultural Memory and Japanese Surrealism*

Peter Schwenger, *Fantasm and Fiction: On Textual Envisioning*

Didier Maleuvre, *Museum Memories: History, Technology, Art*

Jacques Derrida, *Monolingualism of the Other; or, The Prosthesis of Origin*

Andrew Baruch Wachtel, *Making a Nation, Breaking a Nation: Literature and Cultural Politics in Yugoslavia*

Niklas Luhmann, *Love as Passion: The Codification of Intimacy*

Mieke Bal, ed., *The Practice of Cultural Analysis: Exposing Interdisciplinary Interpretation*

Jacques Derrida and Gianni Vattimo, eds., *Religion*

The authorized representative in the EU for product safety and compliance is:
Mare Nostrum Group
B.V Doelen 72
4831 GR Breda
The Netherlands

www.ingramcontent.com/pod-product-compliance
Lightning Source LLC
Chambersburg PA
CBHW020919180526
45163CB00007B/2796